NORSE PAGANISM VS CHRISTIANITY

Jayden K. Helman

© **Copyright 2022 by Jayden K. Helman - All rights reserved**.

This document is geared towards providing exact and reliable information in regard to the topic and issue covered.

- From a Declaration of Principles which was accepted and approved equally by a Committee of the American Bar Association and a Committee of Publishers and Associations.

In no way is it legal to reproduce, duplicate, or transmit any part of this document in either electronic means or in printed format. All rights reserved.

The information provided herein is stated to be truthful and consistent, in that any liability, in terms of inattention or otherwise, by any usage or abuse of any policies, processes, or directions contained within is the solitary and utter responsibility of the recipient reader. Under no circumstances will any legal responsibility or blame be held against the publisher for any reparation, damages, or monetary loss due to the information herein, either directly or indirectly.

Respective authors own all copyrights not held by the publisher.

The information herein is offered for informational purposes solely and is universal as so. The presentation of the information is without contract or any type of guarantee assurance.

The trademarks that are used are without any consent, and the publication of the trademark is without permission or backing by the trademark owner. All trademarks and brands within this book are for clarifying purposes only and are owned by the owners themselves, not affiliated with this document.

Table of Contents

Introduction 1

Chapter One: Between Myth and Reality 5

  1.1 Do fairy tales exist for children? 5

  1.2 Fairy tales and myths 8

  1.3 Snorri's deception? 16

Chapter Two: The genesis of the two families of gods 19

  2.1 Asi and Vani 19

  2.2 The sovereign gods. Odin 27

  2.3 The gods of war. Thor and the fertility gods. Freyr ...37

  2.4 The important gods. Loki 43

Chapter Three: The spread of a buried culture 49

  3.1 The advent of Christianity and its consequences 49

  3.2 Clash between paganism and Christianity.
  Neopaganism 53

  3.3 Instrumentalizations of myth: from storytelling to
  Nazi ideology 91

  3.4 The militarization of a myth. 94

Conclusions 99

Bibliography 102

INTRODUCTION

In studying the religious cultures of the northern peoples, one must keep in mind the limitations of the sources that have come down to us, which very often speak indifferently of Nordic mythology and Germanic mythology, confusing the terms of a specific historical issue. On the whole, the data that we possess on Germanic mythology are indirect sources, in particular reports from Latin historians such as Tacitus, while as far as Nordic mythology is concerned, the documentation is very copious, but not before the 12th century, thus collected and transmitted after the acquisition of writing, an event connected with the preaching and spread of Christianity.

As far as Nordic mythology is concerned, one of the major sources is Snorri Sturluson's *Edda, which makes* explicit references to sources that have come down to us only partially. It is a collection of songs on mythological and epic subjects, probably dating from earlier times than the time of their writing and collection, but with obvious signs of chronological disparity between them. Snorri carries considerable weight in Icelandic literary tradition not only for his research, which orders the historical, literary, and mythological traditions of his country but also as a writer and poet. The *Edda*, the most significant of his works, is presented as a treatise aimed at the professional education of literati. The work contains two separate books that find their unity in their common purpose: the *Gylfaginning* "The Deception of

Gylfi," the *Skáldskaparmál* "The Poetic Language," a veritable technical manual where rhetorical and stylistic figures of the poetic tradition are clarified based on cultural and mythological references drawn largely from the *Gylfaginning*. The work is structured according to a rationalistic clarification of the texts of the ancient poetic and mythical tradition, but without the author making a real distinction between the poetic-literary tradition and the religious tradition, and this apparent confusion of the mythical and epic planes leads to misinterpretations about the importance Snorri gives to the Latin-Christian currents imported into Iceland. This "misunderstanding" ascribes to the scholar a view of ancient religion where the gods would be nothing more than powerful rulers or heroes of the past, who had succeeded, by wisdom or valor, to attribute to themselves divine nature, generalizing interpretative forms that are not reflected in the concrete analysis of the work.

An important scholar of the Germanic peoples was Georges Dumézil, who analyzed the composition of the Scandinavian pantheon and the myths surrounding it critically, without getting carried away by mythic history. He devoted his work to consolidating the comparative religious history, social history, and cultural history of the Indo-European peoples as a sister science to the comparative Indo-European linguistics born in the Romantic Age, succeeding in gaining insights into the ancient history, basic structure, and further development of Indo-European cultures. In his studies, Dumézil emphasizes how religious tradition is important for understanding the mentality and collective organization of a particular social group, trying not to be influenced by our prior knowledge. To do this, in part, we must rely on myths, that is, traditional tales passed down orally that, viewed from a modern point of view, might appear to be simple children's fables, but which conceal a more complicated and profound structure of which we have an overall framework thanks to Russian anthropologist and formalist Vladimir J. Propp, who laid the groundwork for the study of what we now call the "literary genre of the fairy tale." Such a study allows us to analyze the myths of this particular population and the formation of the pantheon, highlighting how each polytheistic religion generated stories that we can compare and contrast: a comparison that leads us to recognize how figures, once religious, are now considered mere subjects of fairy tales and in some cases works of art.

The goal of this thesis is to provide a historical-philosophical insight into a culture that has been little studied to date, to critically analyze the formation of Scandinavian society through its religious tradition and the transformation of this religion into mythology, and then to be used as the basis for the claims that gave rise to Nazi ideology.

CHAPTER ONE
BETWEEN MYTH AND REALITY

<u>1.1 Do fairy tales exist for children?</u>

When the term "fairy tale" is mentioned, we are immediately ready to associate it with a narrow literary genre that is considered secondary, confined to a certain age group, that of childhood, when it is considered normal to be surrounded by unreal and seemingly meaningless stories, superficial because of the presence of characters and events suitable for a still innocent audience. The distinguishing characteristic of children is precisely "literary credulity," something that allows them to identify with the story completely: something that is very difficult for an adult, since he, constantly wrapped up in reality, is inclined to brand the fantastic narration of the tales told to him when he was a child as a silly fantasy and to disavow the "journeys" undertaken in those imaginary territories. In doing so, one forgets that adults were originally the recipients of the stories, from which they often derived simple escapism and entertainment.

However, we must recognize that defining a fairy tale is one of the most complex things known to contemporary literature, and the questions that scholars still try to provide a correct and complete answer to are always the same: what is a fairy tale? What kind of tale can we call one? By what criteria can a narrative be placed within the fairy tale genre? Questions that will probably never be answered, given the changing nature of the stories belonging to this type of literature; the only possible way is to examine the genre, attempt to understand it, and lay it bare in an attempt to understand what makes it so complex and, therefore, fascinating and mysterious. Yet, to examine a fairy tale is not just to understand the most hidden meanings, but also to come up against a deep-rooted and rich critical tradition that has its roots in the 1920s and Formalism, thanks to the work of Russian Vladimir J. Propp and his subdivision into functions, which goes on to establish itself as a starting point for those who have devoted themselves to the genre in the years that followed.

One of the earliest accounts of the fairy tale genre as an expression of culture popular is a collection by a Neapolitan writer, Giambattista Basile, who wrote in his dialect the work *Il cunto de li cunti overo lo trattenemiento de peccerille*, published between 1634 and 1636. This was a collection of fifty short stories of a popular nature, the aim of which, in origin was to entertain the courts, and among these fairy tales we can find some that later taken up by authors such as Charles Perrault and the Brothers Grimm, fairy tales such as Cinderella or Sleeping Beauty in the Woods. The revival of these fairy tales in the authors cited open a study, particularly by the Brothers Grimm, who did not conceive of the classification into "children's fairy tales" of the stories that were being transcribed, given the persistent existence of stories from earlier historical moments; in fact, their work presents a The retelling of fairy tales from the German folk tradition.

But in fact, why are fairy tales considered so important and told?

Commonly they respond by emphasizing their messages of education and training, yet current psychologists point out that many stories in our culture are symbolic representations of emotions such as fear and abandonment, abuse by the adults, the fear of growing up and autonomy; while others think that fairy tales have their own roots in ancient myths, as Bruno Bettelheim does in his 1976 book *The uses of Enchantmen*, in the which argues that fairy tales, and in particular those of the Brothers Grimm, are the representation Of the myths introduced by Freud. Bettelheim argued that the characters moving in fairy tale scenarios were archetypal figures embodying the contradictory tendencies of man. So why not the history of men as well?

1.2 Fairy tales and myths

Identifying a fairy tale as such turns out to be quite easy, thanks to the fundamental component that is the incipit, through which the mind instantly connects to what Tolkien calls the "realm of *Feeria*," that is, a fairy place where "fairies lead their existence."[1]

E important to note the difference between fable and fairy tale. In common usage, these two terms are often confused or used in place of each other, but in literature, they correspond to two very different types of tales: the fable is a text with a didactic intent, whose protagonists turn out to be exemplifications of human virtues and vices, and whose meaning is explained in the moral placed at the beginning or end of the tale; the fairy tale, on the contrary, involves characters who in the course of the narrative do not stand still, but undergo an evolution that accompanies them throughout its course, all the way to the epilogue, which can often be identified with the so-called "and they lived happily ever after." Another key element is the concept of the fairy tale as a "fantastic tale," but also as a "far-fetched, fable-like" tale, which Tolkien himself defines as "an unreal or unbelievable story or fable." The fairy tale resides in the world of the fantastic and the marvelous, and without these two elements one could not speak of a fairy tale, but only of a tale; the recipient of the story must be well aware that what he or she will hear cannot be realized in real life, given the presence of elements "not to be found at all in our primary world," and it is precisely the imaginative element that

---

[1] J.R.R. Tolkien, Tree, and Leaf, cit. p. 20.

relegates the fairy tale to mere childish entertainment, unlike the way the Brothers Grimm thought of it, as already seen.

The impossibility of placing a fairy tale in a given historical or geographic context allows the immediate evidence of a fundamental factor present in all the tales: the repetition of elements present in all the narratives, which allows us to understand how the existence of a common origin of didactic images used to form narrative patterns is evident (apparently) new. From this point of view, we can rely on the formalist view, which has studied and analyzed the formal elements that constitute a literary text with special attention to language, investigating the technical aspect, the procedure that is placed at the basis of the conception and composition of the story, setting aside the elements considered subjective, and it is in this way of conceiving the literary text that Propp is placed.

Vladimir J. Propp was a Russian linguist and anthropologist whose studies on folklore and structural elements of folk tales form the basis of investigations related to traditional literature. Propp's two main studies on the composition, elements and historical and cultural roots of the fairy tale are:

Morphology of the Fairy Tale (1928), in which he formally classifies the genre of the fairy tale by identifying the immutable functions of the characters and their fundamental characteristics based on convincing empirical documentation;

The Historical Roots of Fairy Tales (consisting of one hundred fairy tales collected by Afanasev in the 1800s), which is a reconstruction of the genesis of the fairy tale in a broader historical and cultural context. In the magic tale, he identifies the creative and authentically popular representation of ancient relations of production and corresponding magical-religious manifestations.

The anthropologist extends the French formalist approach to the study of narrative structure: In the "Propp's Sequences" each sequence represents a typical situation in the unfolding of the plot; in his investigation, the scholar organizes the fairy tales into a definite structure, called "Propp's Scheme" in which he starts from a general analysis by dividing the fairy tale into:

- Initial balance (debut);
- rotation of the initial equilibrium (motive or complication);
- vicissitudes of the hero;
- Restoration of balance (conclusion).

Then the internal composition is analyzed, starting with identifying the characters and their roles. The types of characters he describes can be applied to most stories (literary, theatrical, cinematic, etc...); when dealing with the inclusion of character traits in his outline, Propp makes a detailed analysis:

- hero, generally embodied by the protagonist who, after accomplishing a feat, triumphs (he can be a researcher, adventurer, or victim);
- Antagonist, the hero's opponent, the villain;
- false hero, the anti-hero who replaces the hero with deception;
- principal, who invites the hero to go on the mission;

- mentor, the hero's guide, who gives him a magical gift;

- helper, those who help the hero complete the mission;

- Princess, ultimate love prize for the hero;

- ruler, who instructs the hero to identify the false hero and then rewards the real one.

In Propp's study, it is pointed out that different roles can be played by several characters, so one character can play several roles (a witch is killed at the beginning of the tale and her daughter replaces her in the role of the antagonist; the king can be the instigator, but also the hero's helper or the hero himself), however, it is also pointed out that not all fairy tales or myths unfold in all 31 functions, only their precise order being necessary and not their total presence. Thus, the composition of the plot is nothing more than the sum of all the functions necessary for the story being told, placed according to a predetermined sequence.

There are mainly two basic functions that motivate adventures:

- The ban, which prevents the hero from performing a specific action during his adventure occurs in the episode described in the chapter *Harbardhr's Magic Carme* of *The Eddic Songbook*, tell of Norse heroes, where the protagonist of the song is *Thôrr* who, in an attempt to be ferried by a man, who was none other than his father *Odhinn*, to the other side of the strait, engages in a heated argument with the ferryman, who introduces himself under the name of *Harbardhr* and denies him passage.

- The infraction, which occurs as a consequence of the prohibition that gives rise to harm and removal by the hero to remedy or seek an alternative solution to his problem, as occurs in the above episode where *Thôrr* is forced to have to choose an earthly route, pointed out to him by the ferryman, to reach his destination.

It should be emphasized that Propp does not only analyze the fairy tale itself as a tale, but in his studies, he starts from the historical origin of the society in which it originated as a "myth" of ancient civilizations. Through his studies, he disproves the heterogeneity of fairy tales by showing that each of them is nothing more than a variation of the others, regardless of cultural origin. The Scandinavian epic is filled with heroic figures, of whom the most illustrious are also familiar figures: handsome, brilliant, young, and most often power-hungry princes attached to their homeland, they belong to the typical representation of "Odinic heroes," but they are not the only figures; the figure of *Loki* himself turns out to be ambiguous, he is presented as the gods' most valuable friend and helper, but he is also their worst enemy, a characteristic that is emphasized at the end of the episodes involving him so that the "bad guy" Loki appears as such only at the end of a long development[2]. We also have the testimony of an entirely different hero, a hero whose birth already has a mythical character: a descendant of giants, disfigured by horrible wounds, loveless whose only ambition is to fight in the service of his masters. He was *Starkaðr*; these two types of heroes showcase the duality of the typical warrior of this people. The giant has been the subject of numerous studies, and various criticisms, showing the

---

[2] G. Dumézil, Loki, Darmstadt, Wiss. Buchgesellschaft, 1959.

various doubts about his figure being too loaded with details. It is supposed that, like the myth of Heracles, the Scandinavian myth may have been enriched with those details over the centuries passing through different moments in history, and thus be nothing more than a sum of all the stories about him. The only tale that follows the hero from birth to death is that of *Saxo*, where precisely there is a change in tone and spirit between the various episodes of his life.

The myth that is reported by Snorri in the Edda is not a reconstruction of facts based on doctrinal consistency; his work is the result of his gifts as a writer combined with his attitude toward the subject matter; the writer appears more inclined to get involved with the myth rather than to analyze it. Using the words of Carl Gustav Jung, one could say that Snorri is unable to free himself from the archetypal basis of his representations and therefore "continues" the myth, reproduces it, and varies it with legitimacy; one could use, to define the work employed by Snorri, Károly Kerènyi's concept of "variation on a theme," where the theme is the fundamental mythic idea and the variation is the concrete mythological realization of it in time and tradition, or the symbolic deepening of an aspect of mythology, the possible figure of an archetypal symbol. Mythological ideas encapsulate in itself something more than can be thought of "non-mythologically." And it is Snorri's fundamental faculty to think mythologically.

We are not in a position to say that Snorri drew on his sources with the nonchalance of one who is concerned with creating a coherent painting in itself, inventing the connections and raping the tradition, creating the beautiful fairy tales told by his grandmother; however, thanks to the Snorrian sources that have come down to us, we can analyze the manner of

Snorri's operations, affirming the author's substantial correctness concerning tradition. It is quite evident that the writer is sensitive to all suggestions of the subject matter; his gift as a creator of myths turns out to be an explanatory "amplifier" in the autonomous terms of mythic thought.

The variations and accommodations of the myth that we can see in the comparison with other sources are not all to be attributed to Snorri, but also to the tradition to which he is heir, and in this regard, reference can be made to Hans Kuhn's conclusion regarding what Eugen Mogk says about Snorri, pointing out that Mogk's criticism of the author is based on erroneous premises since it assumes that Snorri had at his disposal for the composition of the work only the sources known to us; that every myth has a unique form and that our knowledge of ancient languages is better and broader than that of the author himself. This criticism makes sure to attribute to Snorri an interpretation where the gods represent deified human subjects by the attitude of the Christian church, ignoring the spirit of the Edda.

1.3 Snorri's deception?

Assuming that Snorri carried out an operation of "improvement" on the myth he reported and that therefore there are passages within the Edda that are not properly "true" to the Scandinavian historical-religious tradition, we should pause to analyze these aforementioned passages. In analyzing these passages we will realize that, if we leave out the mythological considerations and Norse religion in general, we will realize that the elements, hypothetically inserted by the author, could be consistent with the original mythological thought; could we, therefore, compare Snorri to a kind of demiurge?

As he does, in his work, with *Odhinn*?

The demiurge is a philosophical and at the same time mythological figure, first appearing in Plato's *Timaeus*, which Snorri himself uses to describe the Great Father of the Scandinavian *pantheon*; the figure of the Demiurge, in myth, is the one without whom nothing can be generated. The philosopher does not argue for it rationally, but introduces it as a cosmological hypothesis with a verisimilar character; it is the "artificer and father of the universe," an ordering, shaping force that vivifies matter by giving it form and order, making it the soul of the cosmos: an image analogous to that of *Odhinn* in the myth of *Gylfaginning*[3], or for that matter, to what Snorri does in his attempt to make the narrative tradition coherent in the Edda.

---

[3] Edda passage where the god Ymir gives up his place as a ruler to Odhinn and his brothers who are presented as demiurges and not as creator deities.

It becomes obvious that Snorri cannot be identified in the figure of the mythological Demiurge, like the mythical *Odhinn*. Plato, in addition to the mythological figure, also describes that of a philosophical demiurge, a unified principle capable of clarifying the dualism between the world of ideas and the world of sensible reality; whereas Snorri he could go on to clarify the doubts about what was reported by him and what other scholars believe to be the actual story. This parallelism with the figure of the philosophical demiurge might help us to understand more fully the syncretistic process employed by the author and his *mythologies*, understanding that this type of procedure is consistent with the narrative language introduced by the Edda and characteristic of the Icelandic tradition itself; one might, yes, suppose that Snorri was aware of sources that have not come down to us today, such as the oral tradition, which, although many years had already passed since the sudden disappearance of paganism, was still very much present in Scandinavia in the period in which the author works.

CHAPTER TWO
THE GENESIS OF THE TWO FAMILIES OF GODS

2.1 Asi and Vani

The analysis of the Indo-European tradition has its origins in linguistic study, which has its roots in the 18th century with the work of Anquetil-Duperron, thanks to whom, for the first time in Europe, Sanskrit was able to be read; he was followed by other scholars who, learning and comparing Sanskrit with other languages, such as Latin and Greek, noticed obvious similarities in a structure going on to develop a true comparative grammar of Sanskrit, Persian, Greek, Latin, Gothic, Lithuanian and German languages. It could then be hypothesized that there was a common language underlying these individual idioms, and the term "Indo-European" was coined to define this basic linguistic unit. This hypothesis led to the conclusion that if there was a language, there was also a people who spoke it, and so people began to search within cultural expressions for traces of these "original people. ",. One of the most important scholars of Indo-European civilizations was, as previously mentioned, Georges Dumézil.

Dumézil, known for his theories on the society, ideology, and religion of ancient Indo-European peoples, reports in *The Fates of the Warrior* that a poet wrote: "The country that has no legends is doomed to freeze to death," thus decreeing the death of those peoples who do not possess myths; which is plausible in that the function of the particular class of legends examined by the scholar is precisely that of expressing the ideology by which that society lives, of keeping alive not only its values and ideals that have been pursued generations but first and foremost its being, its structure, its elements, ties, balances, tensions that constitute it, rules and practices without which all would be lost. These myths can belong to different types, and as far as their origin is concerned, some are extracted from real situations or episodes, more or less stylized and embellished to be presented as examples to be imitated; others are nothing but literary fiction that sees, in the characters, the embodiment of concepts important to the ideology and show correlation with other concepts. As for the setting and the cosmic dimension of the scenes, some are developed in bounded space and the few centuries of national experience recall a past or a future and inaccessible areas of the world and see the presence of gods, giants, monsters, and demons; others, on the other hand, are content to speak of ordinary men, family matters and plausible times, but all these stories have the same vital function and origin: the fantasy that in those periods was intended for adults because it was held as the foundation of their history.

The comparative study of the oldest Indo-European civilizations, which lasted for about thirty years, had to take into account this variety of myths and their functional unity. In particular, it soon became clear that the Romans do not turn out to be a people without mythology, but rather it could be argued that among them mythology, very ancient mythology dating back to Indo-European times, was unified with theology until it survived in the form of history. This could be demonstrated through several instances that include a narrative and characters, which the Hindus and Germans place exclusively in the divine world, but which in Rome appear to refer exclusively to men who existed. Roman ideology thus offers a vision on two parallel planes: on the one hand, a simple and clear-cut theology on all points on which we have much information and which defines and hierarchizes society; on the other hand, we find an origin story that unfolds through adventures of men who, because of their characteristics and function, are called gods. The Roman evolution of mythology sees the three functions theologically expressed in the hierarchy of the gods of the Precapitular Triad.

In Scandinavian mythology, the main gods are divided into two families, the *Asi* and the *Vani*, and the coexistence of these two groups of deities constitutes the fundamental problem of historical-religious research, which finds itself lacking in didactic texts capable of providing a general differential definition of the two families. Yet, the distinction described to us in the stories is so sharp that a general distinction is nevertheless made. We see that the most prominent *Asi* are *Odhinn, Thôrr,* and *Tŷr,* while the main Vani is found in the figures of *Njördhr, Freyr,* and *Freyja.* The latter three are the main dispensers of wealth, patrons of fertility and pleasure, topographically related to the fields and the sea; while *Odhinn* and *Thôrr* have quite different functions between them: the former is the wizard, the lord of runes, head of all divine society, lord and protector of heroes, whether living or dead; the latter is the hammer god and enemy of giants. We know that the two divine families live in agreement and are associated in prayers and worship by men, which is often expressed through a hierarchy of three, where the *Asians* appear superior to the *Dwarves*: *Odhinn*, *Thôrr*, and *Freyr*, who generically summarize the needs of human society and with whom mythology associates the "three great divine jewels forged by the dwarves for a challenge from the evil Loki": the magic ring of *Odhinn*, the *Mjöllnir* hammer of *Thôrr* and the golden-bristled boar of *Freyr*. The hierarchy we also find about the ownership of the dead, where *Odhinn* is entitled to the noblemen and half of the war dead, *Thôrr to the* servants, and *Freyja* (*Freyr*'s twin sister) to the other half of the war dead and the women. Yet in several passages of the Eddic poems, in two texts of Snorri and in four stanzas of the *Völuspâ*, where divine history is traced, we are presented with a division of the two groups in the distant past, a division that had led to a war that ended with the more reasonable *Vani* joining the *Asi*, while the rest of them survived outside the obligation of worship; as to this war and subsequent peace, we can rely on Snorri's account, which contains the time-warped memory of migration, from the shores of the Black Sea to Scandinavia, complete with a struggle between the worshippers of different groups of gods, *Asi* and *Vani*, a struggle that ended with the merger of the two peoples and the two pantheons. This doctrine was prevalent at the time of the Indo-European invasion of the region. We see that from the account we can perceive the differences between the two religious hierarchies: the religion of the *Vani* is the oldest, linked to an agricultural and all in all peaceful and backward society, while the religion of the *Asi* refers to a warrior and more 'spiritual' civilization. This initially was a fundamental theory, now called historicism, formulated by the Romans.

New studies oppose this view, although it is not denied that different civilizations overlapped in Scandinavia, nor that

Scandinavian religion evolved profoundly over the centuries, it is doubted that the division between *Asi* and *Vani* refers to a contrast in behavior. Rather, it would be a consequence of the Germanic invasion, harking back to a pre-existing original unity. Dumézil discards the possibility that the duality of the *Asians* and the *Vani* could have been the consequence of these kinds of events or, even, of evolution. He argued that these groups were two complementary terms of a single religious and ideological structure, in which the existence of one presupposes the existence of the other, and that the initial war serves to justify the final coexistence. Dumézil's objections to the historicizing theory are mainly threefold:

Neither the *Völuspâ* nor the *Skâldskaparmâl* places the narrated events geographically, speaking in the myths of an imprecise time and space. When Snorri looks for connections between the myth and story in *Ynglingasaga* alone act somewhat like those Irish monks who drew their arguments from puns and assonances between local names and names from the Bible or in Greco-Roman culture, for this reason, *Asi* comes from Asia, *Vani* from Vana-kvisl, the Don, but with these premises, it cannot be said with certainty that Snorri was aware of a Gothic tradition of migration from the Black Sea. In these contradictory or at any rate inconsistent representations, traces of different religious views can be discerned, thus noting that Snorri operates, on the structure of the tales, a kind of narrative continuity, a chronological succession.

Even assuming that the distorted historicity of the events of the *Asi-Vani* war is located in Asia, at the mouth of the Don, and that after the conclusion of hostilities *Odhinn* leads the *Asi*, who have since integrated the *Vani, in* Scandinavia, in *Upland, there* would be an inconsistency in the superimposition of a Germanic culture on a local one, which is attested between Germany and Scandinavia, but not in Russia. So it can be said that while preserving Snorri's idea about war, the same cannot be said about geographical location, where he says the false by placing the events in Russia. In contrast, however, in the theologian, Adam Di Bremen's text, *History of the Archbishops of the Church of Hamburg*, completed around 1075-1076, names of peoples, kings, and careful descriptions of movement from one place to another are given with meticulous precision.

All three sources (*Völuspâ, Ynglingasaga,* and *Skâldskaparmâl*) appear to be full of details about the phases of the war and the stipulations of peace, and some picturesque indications, which are by no means to be classified as history, but go into the sphere of myth, are neglected by historicists by considering them secondary, even though the bulk of the text speaks of it. For this reason, one cannot neglect the structure of a source by destroying what one does not consider useful and then reusing what is considered useful for one's purposes.

Snorri's account does not seem, however, to contain a religious thought, but we can observe that one detail or several details, apparently meaningless to the author, go meaning in the folklore of peoples far from Scandinavia. Dumézil points out the commonality of language between the Scandinavians and the Germans, who spoke Indo-European languages, deformed to a small degree by local vocabulary; this commonality implies in representations and organization (hence ideology) a similarity, and religion is the main expression of this. Thus in the presence of a myth of the Scandinavians.

legitimate, before denying its meaning and antiquity, to consider whether the religion of more conservative Indo-European-speaking peoples does not present a homologous belief or narrative.

In Indo-European religions, we know that a small number of deities were grouped by rituals and invocations, they were distributed on three levels that summarized the whole of society. Regarding the tripartition of deities employed by Dumézil, it should be borne in mind that the scholar affirms the illegitimacy of enclosing myths in restrictive schemes, trying to narrow and synthesize their substance and sometimes distort them. Indeed, in doing so, one may risk preserving non-fundamental features by pointing to them as characteristics and neglecting, instead, fundamental features. It must always be remembered that for those populations the entire mythological production is not seen as fanciful, but is part of the real tradition. Therefore, when analyzing a divine hierarchy, one must take into account the messages and lessons that the tales are meant to convey by lowering the risk of error.[18] In particular, regarding the two groups in Scandinavian mythology, we see that in the *Völuspâ the* main gods are hierarchically ordered in this tripartition, which distributed the deities into:

- priests;
- warriors;
- farmers.

Thus, it is hypothesized that the functional tripartition of deities as a mirror of society goes back to the prehistoric past and represents in the Germanic/Scandinavian variant a fundamental archaism preserved over time, although, since warfare was a major factor in society in this people, it is placed above the priestly caste and consequently the tripartition is different from other peoples:

- *Odhinn*, militarized and flanked by *Týr who* is a war god, fearless, with power over victory, although his figure never appears as that of a fighter, except for the sacrifice of the hand to cheat *Fenrir*, thus neglecting the figure of *Týr* as the god of law and identifying him as justice in the battle itself.

  We see in Cicero that this characteristic can also be found in Mars, who takes for himself the bravest and most victorious in battle while condemning cowards and those who run away from warn the second function is placed *Thôrr*, whom Latin writings place metaphorically in parallel with *Hercules* or the god *Vulcan*;

- In the third, the presence of a pair *Njördhr* and *Freyr* (father and son) or the twins *Freyr* and Freyja, are rulers and protectors of the people.

Mythology also associates these three figures with the tripartition of souls, as mentioned earlier, which are brought by the *Valkyriors* into the *Volhöll*, where the souls of the warriors will lead an existence roughly similar to that lived among mortals while waiting for the best 800 of them to join *Odhinn*'s troops to face *Fenrir*.

2.2 The sovereign gods. Odin

Regarding the first deity of the main triad, we note that there appears to be no difference between the figure of *Odhinn* that can be inferred from the Eddic poems and the one described by Snorri. He turns out to be the chief of the gods, the king who will rule them until the end of time and who especially protects human kings and their power, but at the same time, he is also the god who demands their blood in sacrifice at the moment when the king's virtue is no longer sufficient for the people to prosper. In his leadership figure, he is the one who suffers the most from the great drama of divine history, starting with the killing of his son *Baldr*, which he foresaw and could not prevent; in fact, he is the seer, a gift that is symbolically expressed using mutilation, voluntary: he is monocle because he pledged an eye in the source of all knowledge.

Included in his dimension are runes, the magic of letters, and the most powerful secrets, through which more things can be known than any other being in the world; this mysterious wisdom of his results is inseparable from the equally mysterious poetic inspiration, which which we see in the myth of the wise *Kvasir*: born after the peace between *Asians* and *Vanians*, he was the wisest of beings created from the saliva of the gods. When *Kvasir* died, the two dwarves who killed him mixed his blood with honey, giving rise to a drink that is often found in the stories of these peoples: mead, which was later stolen by *Odhinn* so that it would give *Asians* and humans poetic ability.

The sagas often show him as the arbiter of fights and judge of death for all who dare to cross their swords against his; his men are divided into two representations: the *berserkir* warriors, who seem to partake of his gifts of metamorphosis, of his magic, and who in the sagas are brigands without morals or shame; and then the noble, chivalrous so-called "Odinic," of whom the *Sigurdhr* of the Scandinavian Nibelungen cycle is the most famous example. These heroes are chosen by the god himself and upon their departure are taken from the *Valkyrie* and are led for eternity to the life of fighters. The *Grimnismâl* describes the sojourn of the god and his favorites, who await the day of battle for the end of the world. According to tradition, to "get to *Odhinn*" in the afterlife, it is necessary to be marked, before death, with the mark of the god himself; the mark consists of a spearhead cut; another method is hanging. In archaic culture, the glory had to be earned, and the means used to achieve that end was war. In the myths describing *Odhinn*'s abode, men who have fallen on the battlefield devote much of their time to lavish banquets, and when they are not engaged in this they engage in endless fighting. *Odhinn*'s chosen ones do constitute a "band," a society of men, the type of idea that had spread about the Vikings, but which turned out to be as old as the Germanic world.

Yet, little is known about the ruler of Scandinavian religion except for a few nicknames of uncertain interpretation, until modern folklore links him to practices or beliefs that concerned rural and agricultural life. In 1876 Karl Nikolaj Henry Petersen's thesis opened a crisis by claiming that *Odhinn* came from the religions of the north, while some radical scholars argue that his figure penetrated Scandinavia by coming from the south. Others admit the plurality of race, Scandinavian-Germanic, arguing, however, that his origins in these territories are humble, almost insignificant. The improbability that this figure is of Germanic origin also arises because the name itself, *Odhinn*, does not turn out to be common Germanic, but only West Germanic and Nordic. A reliable thesis is the one that it can be placed with the Goths, with a word derived from *Wut*, one of the Scandinavian appellations, *Gautr*, and the location in Gotland of most of the place names encapsulated in its name. Of particular relevance, also turns out to be the position taken by archaeologist Oscar Montelius. Having already extensively emphasized that *Odhinn* is the great god of runes and runic magic, with Montelius we come up against a fact that should not be underestimated. Runic writing is a relatively recent invention, imported from the southeast, according to some, or with a derivation from the south, according to a more accredited opinion. Hence its existence after the Christian era and the massive influence of the Roman world on the Germanic world. Thus the runes would have been assigned to *Odhinn since he was* already recognized as a magician; moreover, *runar* is a word from ancient Germanic and Celtic that designated magical secrets from the beginning.

The antiquity of *Odhinn* or its function was based on precise arguments based on two more general reasons:

- the breadth and variety of the fields in which the god operates are the first of the reasons. These two characteristics seem to testify to growth, a development; it is assumed that this covering of his varied fields is a symptom of an extension, and there are numerous models proposed to trace the origin of the assumed development: some believe that the god would have been, at first, only a small domestic god or a sorcerer god; others believe that he was the god of the dead or fertility;

- the second reason was formulated during a period of decline for the studies of "comparative mythology," as a reaction to the illusions and excesses of Max Müller's school. He argued for an onomastic correspondence where the Vedic god of the sky, *Dyauh*, the Greek *Zeus*, the Latin *Juppiter,* and the Germanic character who in Old Norse became *Týr meet*. We see that the older and "great god" recurs in the two Mediterranean heirs as well, and if at the Scandinavians as at the Germans this great god subsists, it does not have the importance ascribed to its prototype, since it turns out to be subordinate to *Odhinn in* the same way, since at the time of reference of the documents, he is at the end of a long regress.

These two pieces of evidence are at the heart of the problem: the first is problematic because of the multiplicity of starting points and the hypothetical itineraries in which we have tried to specify its image. These stratifications may present themselves in the reassuring language of history, but they are only the result of reflections that contradict each other, proving that none of them is satisfactory. Generally, one is reduced in admitting foreign influence on the Rhine and the fjords when confronted with the imperial power of Rome or Byzantium, yet it turns out to be unlikely *Týr*, as king of the *Asians*, because there are no resonances of possible influence. Thus, if one admits that the values of the head of the gods, of the world, and the great magician are fundamental and original to the god, then it turns out that at the top of the divine pyramid there has always been *Odhinn* from the beginning; earthly kings are nothing more than correspondents of *Odhinn* among men, while the Roman *Juppiter* is nothing more than a dispenser of victory as ruler.

Jan de Vries points out that *Odhinn*'s name induces us to place a spiritual notion at the center of his being: the Old Norse word from which he derives, *odhr*, and which Adam of Bremen translates as *furor* and corresponds to the German *Wut* and the Gothic *words* "possessed." So this name was intended to identify a god of the "first level." In contrast, about the problem involving the role of the Germanic *Tiuz*, *Týr* is based on a simplistic and erroneous interpretation. In fact, in various provinces of the Indo-European whole, a divine function is ascribed and endorsed by the myths, which illustrate it; we see that the Vedic god *Varuna*, unlike the Indo-European ones, does not surpass the luminous sky, while *Juppiter* and *Zeus* are the deified sky, but he is the topical, personal king of gods and men, and the dazzling god. If you want to compare them, it is better to refer to the rulers *Varuna* or *Mithras*, or the dazzling *Indra*. Thus, if we refer to the "three functions" scheme we see that *Juppiter* occupies the first level, in India, on the other hand, *Dyauh* results outside the scheme and the first level were occupied by *Varuna* and *Mithras*. Under similar conditions, the Indo-European name *Dyeu, Tiuz*, probably does not apply to the homologous god by function, but it seems plausible that the functions of these are secured toward the Germans by a god bearing another name, a new name probably Germanic. We may venture to say, through the study of Indo-Iranian and Roman theology, that in a distorted way the same two-term structure may underlie the duality of *Odhinn* and *Týr*: from the Germanic point of view neither of them is "the oldest," they are extensions of two Indo-European deities. The correspondence between *Odhinn* and *Varuna* is striking: both turn out to be magicians, and the gift of metamorphosis, characteristic of the Norse god, coincides with the *Maya* that the Indo-Iranic god makes use of; *Varuna*'s instantaneous and irresistible grasping, expressed in his laces and knots, coincides with *Odhinn*'s mode of action, which has the gift of blinding, deafening, numbing, and even binding with an invisible lace. That lace is the *her-fjöturr*, "the lace of the army," a spell that essentially paralyzes the combatant. The poets personified this notion in one of the Valkyries: *Helfjötur*.

However, we see that as similar as the varied domains of the two deities are, there are naturally many differences that can be explained by comparing the environments, different geographical locations, and living conditions in which the two religions were practiced. One of these differences in particular reveals an original aspect of ancient Germanic civilizations. One is immediately struck by *Odhinn*'s connection with war, in this world and the *Volhöll*; we can see that he turns out to be a combatant himself very rarely, except in the historicization of the *Ynglingasaga*, where he is referred to as *her-madhr mikill*, "great man of war," and marches from conquest to conquest. In many other instances, however, he is seen to be present in the melees, where he decides on the spot the fate of the battle, expressing his verdict through precise gestures and then casting the lariat on the enemy; thus, although in all this he acts in a manner in keeping with his essence as a ruler and often through purely magical actions, it remains that in these actions warfare turns out to be a constant. The explanation for this peculiarity is obvious: in Germanic ideology and practice, war is a dominant factor. It follows that when they are not fighting, these peoples think about future fighting, and this since childhood.

This character of Germanic society explains the evolution of the Germanic equivalent of the *Mithra-Varuna* duality, *Týr*: thus adopting the view of a Germanic *Mars*, like Tacitus and numerous inscriptions do, to make the *Tiuz* Germanic and the *Týr* Scandinavian, defining him first of all as a god of war. Yet some facts limit us in this definition, showing us that, as a first thing, in preparing for heroic deeds it is to *Thôrr* that the warriors of Tacitus' Germany turn; we may also add, however, that in all Scandinavian literature one would go in vain in search of a passage that portrays *Týr* as a brave fighter occupied in bloody battles, and those few reports that have been assigned to him derive from false etymologies and misinterpreted facts. The only feasible example given to us by Snorri is one connected with a sacrifice: where we see that the god deliberately introduces his right hand into the jaws of the wolf Fenrir. Dumézil compares the Scandinavian religious tradition with the Roman one, and he comes across parallelism that relates precisely to the figure of the gods of the first group: in the Roman tale Gaius Mucius Scaevola becomes the one-armed man by burning his right hand before the Etruscan king because "my hand has erred and now I punish it for this unforgivable mistake"; thus he put the his right hand in a brazier where the fire of sacrifices was burning and did not remove it until it was completely consumed. From that day on, the brave Roman nobleman would take the surname Scevola (the left-handed). The episode is complementary to the epic scene above, which features *Týr* as brave, and the mutilation of *Odhinn*. On both sides, we find the relationship between the diptych of actions or intentions and the diptych of mutilations: the single eye fascinates and immobilizes the opponent; the right hand deliberately sacrificed to guarantee a claim causes the opponent to create that claim, on which the salvation of society depends.

Finally, we must dwell on a further character that links *Mars* and *Týr*: the *thing*, that is, the assembly of the people. J. de Vries notes that generally too much importance is given to the warrior character of the god and little recognition is given to its value for Germanic law. It is important to keep in mind the Germanic point of view, in which there is no contradiction between the concept of the god of battles and the god of law, and war is seen as a decision obtained between two fighting parties and guaranteed by precise rules of law. One can also see this equality of concepts in Tacitus, who describes the assembly of the Germanic peoples as a place where people stand armed and to show assent they shake their axes; a few centuries later in Scandinavia, one can see the same spectacle where people gather armed and to assent, they wave swords or axes or even beat their weapons on shields. The *thing* turns out to be a test of strength between families or groups, where the most numerous and the most threatening impose their preferences, and well used the right constitutes a victory just as in the mythical episode in which *Týr* turns out to be the hero.

The Asi looked at each other and it seemed now that the difficulty was double, no one wanted to offer his hand until Týr stretched out his right hand and put it in the wolf's mouth. And when the wolf pointed his feet and made force the lasso became harder, and the harder he strained the harder the rope cut into his body. Then everyone laughed, except Týr. He lost his hand.[4]

The voluntary mutilation and its function are in stark relation to *Odhinn's* seer function and mutilation. The loss of *Týr's* hand in a fraudulent pardon process that qualifies him as a "juristic god," aimed, however, not at pacification of one

---

[4] Snorri Sturluson, Edda, cit. p. 83.

another, but to the annihilation of one another, leads him not to be called the "peacemaker of men." The two mutilations are seen as a clear symbol of the manifestation of the abilities of the deity: the seer who captivates and the leader of the procedures turn out to be a sensitive expression of a theologian that gives foundation to the existence of two higher deities.

Looking at the Vedic religion, we notice that it does not only present *Mithras* and *Varuna* as sovereign gods; this religion presents two groups of sovereign gods:

1. *Mithras, Aryaman,* and *Bhaga* cooperate in the work and with the legal and just spirit expressed in the first of the group; *Varuna, who* results solitary with his rigor and in magic. The presence of two auxiliaries at *Mitra*'s side is easily understood: *Aryaman,* who bears in his name *Arya and* is associated with the protection of the *Arya* nationality and ensures its durability and cohesion (marriage alliance, gifts, hospitality); *Bhaga,* whose name means "the Part" or "the Attribution," who ensures the peaceful distribution of *Arya* goods. In addition, we see that Vedic Indians are little concerned about what may arise after death, which also rarely appears in the hymns, thus coming to lack some sort of description of the duties of *Aryaman,* which we know continued even in the underworld, where he turns out to be the king of a category of ancestors: the "Fathers." But while there is little mention of the latter detail, instead *Bhaga* is invoked by the poets in the hymns; he is one of a group of maimed, whose maiming is as paradoxical as that of *Odhinn* (seer because he is monocle) and *Týr* (patron of the procedural quibbles of the *thing* after surrendering his arm for a pardon procedure): *Bhaga* distributes the "parts," is blind and is flanked by *Savitr* who sets everything in motion and

has lost both hands, and *Pushan*, the protector of pets, who has lost his teeth. The image of *Bhaga* references the blindfolded Western figure of *Tyche* or Fortuna, the distributor of fortunes.

2.3 The gods of war. Thor and the fertility gods. Freyr

The gods forming the second and third groups of the functional triad do not present as many difficulties as do the sovereign gods. The *Thunraz* of the Germans mentioned by Tacitus was a *Hercules*, as indeed was the *Thôrr* of Scandinavian mythology: enormously strong-a strength he can increase with the help of a belt and magic gloves-he spends most of his time on journeys, alone or in the company of his servant *Thjalfi*, looking for giants to strike down; his weapon, *Mjöllnir*, like Indra's *Vajra*, is a celestial weapon, the lightning accompanying "thunder," which provides the name for the god. Defender of divine society and to this he certainly owes the place of honor he occupied in the temple of *Upsala*, when it was described by Adam of Bremen:

In this temple, which is entirely decorated in gold, the people worship statues of three gods: in the center of the hall has your throne *Thôrr*, the most powerful of them, to the right and left have placed *Wotan* and *Fricco*. They have the following meanings: *Thôrr*, they say, rules over the atmosphere, governing thunder, lightning, winds and rains, good weather, and the produce of the fields. The second, *Wotan*, i.e., Fury, is the God of war and infuses men with courage against enemies. The third is *Fricco* who gives mortals peace and pleasure of the senses.[5]

We can see that when he is not present in the *Asi*'s enclosure the great dangers, but it is enough for the gods to utter his name to invoke him, menacingly, in a state that makes him

---

[5] Adam Di Bremen, History of the Archbishops of the Church of Hamburg, Turin, UTET, De Agostini Libri, 2013, p. 307.

similar to his monstrous adversaries. Nothing can hold him back.

The diversity of *Thôrr* and *Odhinn*'s respective relationships with warriors stands out from various data: first of all *Odhinn*'s insulting phrase in the *Hârbarhsljôh*, which attributes to himself "the nobles who fall in combat" and to *Thôrr* "the race of servants"; if this is but the caricature of a belief, and J. De Vries believes that the poet substituted *thrall for* a the less ignominious notion, a kernel of truth nevertheless results in this dual formula confirmed by the fact that there appear to be no "heroes of *Thôrr*," while there are in large numbers those Odinic and their variety are remarkable. Excluding the warfare field, the essential distinction between *Odhinn* and *Thôrr* is expressed in the Eddic poem of the *Hârbardhsljôdh*, where the two gods are exchange insolence and boasting, many of which serve as definitions. In this poem one has Wanted to see a document from which a conflict of cults, a rivalry of groups shines through religious, the regression or advancement of one of the two gods in the favor of the faithful. Yet, we can assert that there is no rivalry between religious groups, but the poet exploits the pattern of dialogue to better bring out the different natures of the two gods and the different, sometimes contrary, services that they render in different places of the same stable theological structure.

According to other studies, the superstitions of modern Scandinavian folklore, the surviving of old agrarian cults and the evidence that Lappish traditions have delivered to the Axel Olrik's analysis of the ancient folk religion of the Norwegians wants to shift the center of gravity of the character and prove that *Thôrr* had been something other than a warrior. While the Edda depicts him as a man in the strength of age, for the Lappish tradition, by some Norwegian folk expressions, he was a red-bearded elder; the names given to him by the Lapps reproduce or translate Scandinavian names of a uniform and the least Eddic type possible: Hora Galles, "the good man Tor," an expression noted in folk songs of the late Middle Ages, *Agja* "the grandfather," *Adschiegads* "the little father," *Toraturos bodne* (the first word contains *Thôrr*'s very name and the second, "old man," is taken from the Scandinavian *bôndi* "farmer, head of household"); in southern Sweden, *Thôrr,* the thunder, is called *go-bonden*, "the good farmer," by farmers, *Korn-* or *âker-bonden*, "the good grain man." These Swedish names relate to the Lappish cult, where *Thôrr* is a fertility god who gives rain or sunshine according to the needs of the land, and ripens and protects crops.

In the ninth century, to define *Thôrr*, Adam of Bremen associates him with thunder, wind, rain, and crops, while linking a third of the triad, *Freyr*, to peace and pleasure and reserving for the first, "sovereign" *Wodan*, all of *Thôrr*'s properly warlike aspect. Later, speaking of the *Upsala* sacrifices, he limits the god's competence: *si pestis et fames imminent, Thor idolo libatur*[6], so the god gave the Swedish peasants the atmospheric elements of a good harvest. Axel Olrik argues that the Lappish sacrifice combines the offering to the earth, "that it may nourish the herds, drive disease away from them, and give the beasts vigorous mating," and the offering to the thunder, "that it may spare the beasts and the people and send fruitful rain." Yet, it is through rain, the happy outcome of the atmospheric battle, and the deeds of his hammer, that *Thôrr* promotes agriculture and not through some power over germination.

In the historicizing perspective of the *Yngligasaga*, Snorri makes *Njördhr* and *Freyr* the first and second successors after *Odhinn*'s death, describing their reign:

"*Njördhr* became the ruler of the Swedes and took care of the sacrifices. The Swedes made him king. He received taxes from them. In his time there was excellent peace and crops of all sorts, so abundant that the Swedes believed that *Njördhr* had power over the crops and the A wealth of men."

"*Freyr* received kingship after *Njördhr*. He was elected king of the Swedes and received taxes from them. He was popular and lucky in crops like his father. *Freyr* established a great temple in *Upsala* and also established his capital there and concentrated his rents, lands, and currency."

Gylaginning, which turns out to be closer to mythological characters, provides characteristics for each of the three Realms:

Njördhr: dwelt in the sky, the place called *Nôatûn*. He has power throughout the winds and calms the sea and fire; he was to be invoked for navigation and fishing and being a possessor of riches they invoked him to attract earthly goods. He later had two children, a boy *Freyr* and a girl *Freyja*, the most beautiful and powerful.

Freyr, the most famous of the *Asians*, had power over rain, the sun, and the earth; therefore, it was good to invoke him for crops and peace. He also has power over the wealth of men.

Freyja is the most famous of the *Asìne*, owns the abode in heaven called *Fôlkvangar,* and possesses half of the dead, those who do not go to *Odhinn*. She is given the title of honor *frû* (Frau) by which noblewomen are called. She loves love poetry and it was good to invoke her for love.

Different tales, poetic periphrases, and other data complement the depictions of these two figures, but the basic characters have been listed above; we could broaden the field about *Freyja* and *Freyr* since it turns out to be broader than Snorri says. In Indo-European and Vedic times, the third function included, in addition to fertility and wealth, other characteristics such as beauty, sexual desire, and pleasure. The Scandinavian twins retain these characteristics completely: regarding *Freyja*, the witch *Hundla* and *Loki* insinuate that she had many lovers, although mythology does not record precise adventures confirming such mischief; like *Isis,* however, she traveled the entire world in search of her lost husband, sowing golden tears. Further characteristic, according to tradition, is that before they entered the *Asi,* the two brothers lived as spouses according to the customs of the *Vani*, a characteristic that indicates the different sexual morality between the *Vani of the* 'third function' in the free state and the *Asi.*

The character of *Njördhr* is famous in the history of Germanic religions because Tacitus reported her, but with female gender: she is the *Nerthus* of the XL chapter of *Germania,* honored by a kind of amphizionia of small peoples in southern Denmark. Peoples who, taken alone, had nothing special, but who had a common cult, that of *Nerthus,* the Earth Mother; they believed that this deity intervened in human affairs by circulating in a chariot from one tribe to another. The dispenser of joy and peace possessed the characteristics of the Scandinavian god, and *Njördhr was* often derived from this deity, assuming that the cult was is extended northward from the geographical position in which Tacitus places it; as for the difference of the sexes, it is explained in a variety of ways, though unsatisfactory. Most likely this is a further attestation of a fact not uncommon in the marine folklore of Scandinavia; in any case, the god's specialties to the sea, not as a cosmic element, but as a navigational place bearing wealth and nutritional fishing, are worth noting: lord of the winds on land and sea, and protector of fishing boats; it is to these two terms that the definition of his Lappish transposition is reduced, and Dumèzil finds in a collection of Norwegian folklore a survival of *Njördhr* and his function even in 18th-century folk beliefs. This maritime character of the god gave rise to a famous myth: his unhappy marriage to the eponymous goddess of the Scandinavian lands, *Skadhi*, the daughter of a giant with whom he agreed on peaceful cohabitation. This agreement stipulated that they would spend nine nights in the mountains and nine nights on the coast because one could not stand the other's element and vice versa. Thus, after the nights on the coast, *Skadhi* returned to the Alps of Scandinavia without coming down.

The connection with the sea of at least one of the masters of the third function may have Indo-European roots: consider, for example, that the Greek Dioscuri, despite considerable differences, are also the protectors of sailors. In addition to this peculiarity, we know of *Freyr* that he possessed a magical ship, which he can fold and put in his pocket and which goes faster than any other. *Njördhd* and *Freyr are* closely united, they have the same fruitful action, the same love of peace, and the formulas associate them indistinctly. It should be noted, however, that Scandinavians over time tend to stop expressing the identity of function and do so by making *Njördhr the* father of *Freyr*. *Freyr* is the hero or at any rate the beneficiary of a pleasant tragicomedy, the *Skîrnismâl*, in which some have wanted to see the trace of a *hieros gamos* ritual. Enamored to the point of decay with the giantess *Gerdhr*, the god sends his servant to her who will attempt to win her over on his master's behalf and relents only when the servant casts some less than reassuring "fates" against her. One of the most interesting details of the poem is that it makes *Freyr* a doomed man the moment he gives his sword to the servant as payment for him to fulfill his mission. This gift will never be returned, leaving him unarmed in the duel against the enigmatic Beli; Snorri emphasizes that this sword shines precisely because of its absence and is enough to give him the title of "warrior god," as those who sought to mitigate the fundamental difference between *Asi* and *Vani* often did. *Freyr*'s sword is contrasted with *Odhinn*'s lariat, the bow of the god *Vali* and *Ullr*, and *Thôrr*'s hammer; the attempts to make *Njördhr* and *Freyr* warrior gods are based on a poor understanding of the rules of poetic artifice.

2.4 The important gods. Loki

A further look at the Vedic religion leads us to note that the poets constantly speak of demonic beings to celebrate the victories of the gods and gain new ones. In the *Brahmanas* they order such portrayal, pitting gods against demons as two rival peoples though related, telling of various conflicts but never of the "end," and no character is presented as the leader of demonic forces acting anarchically.

The society of the Scandinavian gods, on the other hand, presents an extremely peculiar figure: *Loki*, intelligent and cunning but amoral and eager to do evil, who represents a demonic element among the *Asians*. Many among the assailants of *Ragnarok* (the wolf *Fenrir*, the great Serpent, and *Hel*) are his children; while among the sons of *Odhinn* we find two tragic figures: *Baldr* and *Hödhr*, whereof the latter only one action is known: the unintentional murder of his brother *Baldr*, and the fact that he is completely blind and unable to take care of himself. *Baldr* brings together in himself the ideal of true justice and genuine goodness, but none of his judgments can be realized since *Týr*, to whom justice is reserved, "is no peacemaker of men." According to Snorri's *Gylfaginning*, *Baldr* allegedly dreamed of his end and turned to the *Asians* for safeguard. Then the goddess *Frigg*, his mother, collected the oaths of everything and being. They all swore never to harm Baldr, but the cunning *Loki* changed his appearance and went to ask the goddess if there was even one thing he had not sworn. *Frigg* revealed to him that to the west of the *Valhöll* a young shoot of wood was growing, the mistitling "mistletoe shoot," which the goddess had deemed too young to make him swear. It was then that the god went and uprooted that sprout and then persuaded *Hödhr* to hurl it at his brother, who was pierced by falling dead. In this episode, *Odhinn* appears the most suffering because he knew the tragic consequences of that death. In the *Völuspâ* the encounter with the witch who prevents *Baldr*'s return from *Hel*'s kingdom is reported:

On their way back, having fulfilled their mission well, the messengers found a witch named Thökk in a cave. They asked her to Weep to remove Baldr from Hel's power. She replied, "Thökk will mourn with dry tears the cremation of Baldr! Neither living nor dead has I taken advantage of the son of man: let Hel keep what he has."

The two events, the tragedy of *Baldr* and the "fate of the gods," have been the subject of studies and a variety of hypotheses. About the second issue, many experts have recognized an influence of Iranian, Zoroastrian eschatology, while *Baldr* is generally interpreted as a god of agrarian ritual, who dies and resurrects, but an influence of the *Attis* or Adonis of the eastern Mediterranean has also been thought of. It can, however, be argued that the Para- and pre-Vedic influence is discernible, and thus that, based on Indo-European data, the Germans and Indo-Iranians organized their accounts of the great struggle.

From what we have been able to analyze, *Loki* is an important god who appears in a variety of stories, yet he turns out to be a god without worship, and in none of the Scandinavian countries does there appear to be a place named after him. So we might come to think that this god may be a fairy tale character (an antagonist or even a false hero, depending on the story being told). Reflecting on the matter, however, we would realize that by removing the character of *Loki*, many stories of *Odhinn* and *Þórr* would have to change shape even though it is unlikely that his absence would deprive the latter of the status of gods. It can be inferred from this that the god *Loki* has a special role in Scandinavian tales: he is the counterpart of the inspirer of the world's great misfortunes, the demonic spirit, the embodiment of the demon of our cosmic age. Thus, considering the drama can be divided into three stages:

1. The demonic *Loki* uses the blind *Hödhr* to eliminate the god *Baldr*, and thus sending him into exile in the *Helheimr* (in the place of *Hel*). To achieve his purpose he makes use of a game that *Baldr* has every reason to regard as harmless, but in the course of which he is killed by the only weapon left that is dangerous to him; he uses a mechanism parallel to that which leads to *Yudhishthira*'s temporary elimination and long exile: the demonic *Duryodhhana* wrests permission from the blind

Dhrtarâshtra to set the scene, where the protagonists are intent on playing a game of which *Yudhishthira* is an avid player but his opponent will use supernatural magic tricks that, once he has been won, force him into exile.

The two main differences concern the specification of the games and the unequal degree of guilt: on the one hand, the Indian blind man knows to what misfortune his action will lead but performs it out of weakness, on the other hand, the Scandinavian blind man who is an unconscious instrument of the wicked man's cunning. These differences allow the essential parallelism to be preserved but would also be sufficient to discard the hypothesis of literary borrowing or influence.

2. The fatal game scene opens a long dark period that should constitute the final part of a cosmic age, since the person responsible would embody, precisely, the evil genius of the present age. The waiting period ends with the final battle, which will see the death of all the representatives of Evil and many of those of Good; the circumstances leading up to the battle are different: in Scandinavia, the battle is engaged by the forces of Evil that had remained chained up to that point; while in the *Mahâbhârata* the survivors among the "good" are the *Pândava*, in the Nordic myth the functional gods die as their opponents and the survivors or reborn are the children of the gods.

3. The former difference is mitigated by the fact that the Indian counterparts of *Baldr* and *Hödhr, Viduna,* and *Dhrtarâshtra* receive in the rebirth new tasks: with the end of the ancient disagreement they become the instruments of *Yudhishthira's* perfect government, so in the rebirth of

the world purified of evil the two sons take the place of the rulers.

The breadth and regularity of the concordance between the two epics seem to solve the problems of *Baldr* and *Hödhr*, and of *Loki* and *Ragnarök*, leading us to discard solutions based on Iranian, Caucasian, or Christian influences and highlighting a vast myth about Good and Evil, which must have already been formed among the Indo-Europeans before the dispersion. The difficulties in describing the figure of *Loki* also lie in the fact that some philological schools turned most theories about the character into ashes. To formulate his profile, it must be kept in mind that antinomies do not hide *Loki*'s personality but can identify a "historical evolution" or a complex and contradictory figure on the model of the Ossetian *Syrdon*.[6]

---

[6] If sickness and hunger loom, Thor offers himself as a liberating idol.

CHAPTER THREE
THE SPREAD OF A BURIED CULTURE

3.1 The advent of Christianity and its consequences

As was expounded in the first chapter, fairy tales mirror the society in which the storytellers lived, but, as Propp points out, every fairy tale, every myth is but a variation of the others regardless of cultural origin. However, we must point out that the stories that have come down to us from people who did not know writing were told to us by third parties, who saw the traditions of the peoples with whom they came in contact according to their morals and beliefs. We must therefore keep in mind that a good deal of ancient literature corresponds to religious tales, which with the advent of monotheism came to constitute a cultural production.

The introduction of Christianity to Denmark and Sweden occurred in the first half of the 9th century, and two hundred years later it was brought to Norway and the western archipelagos; in that period on the one hand the golden age of courtly poets with learned and forced language developed; on the other hand, the 9th and 10th centuries was the age of the Vikings, of simpler and usually stronger anonymous poems that went on to make up the collections of the Edda, probably written between the 9th and 12th centuries and later edited in the 13th century by the Icelandic scholar Snorri Sturluson.

Further traces of the life of the Scandinavian people and religion can be found in the work of Adam Of Bremen, a work that is divided into four volumes in which the Christianization missions inaugurated in 832 are reported; although the theologian never made those journeys himself, he wrote the work relying on the documentary and literary tradition of ancient and medieval texts, and also on oral tradition.

From its beginnings, Christianity has progressively constituted itself against polytheistic religions, although ancient peoples were not aware that they were polytheists, as the term was introduced only by a Jewish thinker in the first century CE (Philo of Alexandria). The term "polytheism," therefore, went to denote a complex of beliefs and rituals that appealed to multiple deities and not to a single god. Polytheism, therefore, was constituted by theopposite category to that of monotheism. Christianity gradually set itself against the classical religions, relegating them to the territory of falsehood and error, later becoming the dominant religion in many parts of the world. Adam of Bremen points out that the inhabitants of the Scandinavian territories "worshipped those who were not gods by nature," and that these gods were not enclosed in temples, nor depicted in statues with human features. The arrival of Christians in the northern lands gave way to conversion missions by religious leaders and monks, whose task was to bring the pagans, who lived in those lands, to "the word of God" by imposing Christianity even through violent persecution campaigns. Another task of these "missionaries" was to bring back the history of the peoples with whom they came in contact, reckoning with a poorly written tradition, from which, however, names of kings who preceded the advent of the

Christian invasion have been derived and who in some cases coincide with figures present in the mythical oral tradition, such as Björn who, according to the aforementioned tradition, was a semi-legitimate king of Scandinavia.

With the spread and establishment of Christianity, ancient religions are remembered as outdated religions, defeated by monotheism and the progress of civilization, according to an evolutionary view to which theologians, Christian philosophers, and the historians of religion themselves contributed. During this evolution, Christianity applied censorship on ancient religions, reducing their gods to characters in generic *mythology*, a component of fantastic tales, and fairy tales. Adam Di Bremen attests that the Germanic religion would be distinguished from other polytheistic religions (such as Roman and Greek) by one very strong trait: the brutality of rituals and more. The theologian reports not only violence during clashes between pagans and Christians, but also human sacrifices and inhumane torture, reporting the words of a king of the Danes:

"Having slaughtered all the others like beasts, sixty priests were kept alive by mockery. Among them was the senior provost of the place who had as his name *Oddar* and was our blood relative. Together with the others, he was thus martyred: with a knife, the skin of each one's head was incised in the form of a cross and his skull laid bare; then, their hands tied behind their backs, the confessors of God were dragged through every center of the Slavs and tormented with beatings or otherwise until they died."

Scenes of this kind recur frequently in the theologian's work, not only in moments where the narrative illustrates events of the war but also in situations of attempts at conversion, such as the one narrated in paragraph 60 of Book Two: when a certain *Volfredo*, an Anglo who preached the love of God, arrived in Sweden and set out to curse the god whom the local pagans called *Thôrr* and shattered his simulacrum that stood in the center of the assembly. At this action, the inhabitants pierced him and then threw his mangled body into a swamp.

3.2 Clash between paganism and Christianity. Neopaganism

The topic of paganism, in general, is very broad and complex. First of all, the very heavy role of Catholic proselytism (much more invasive and fanatical than Orthodox proselytism) during the Middle Ages when the church of Rome in its economic expansion tried at various times to engulf Orthodoxy and, at the same time and in all ways, to obfuscate paganism. With the reboant and continuous proclamations from the papal see against the pagans even "holy" crusading armies were put together to fight the so-called heresies and any other traditional faiths, not acceptable for the latter that they could be put on the same level as an independent and autonomous religion such as Christianity and first of all not granting any alternative for the prevailing creeds in the new northern territories that were being conquered.

In the historical period from 1000 to 1500, any kind of religious competition was considered harmful and was vehemently opposed everywhere and in any case. This naturally led to a strengthening of mutual hatred, not only between the two major Christian centers (Rome and Constantinople) for the grabbing of possible catechumens but also between small local pagan groups, each jealous of its origins and unwilling to come under a new ideological-political regime.

Fortunately, in recent years, very timely and meticulous works have been published on the subject of the Catholic Church and the struggle against paganism, and there has been a realization that the latter faith, primordial and ultimately ecological, is making a comeback throughout Europe despite Catholic claims to Rome as the sole source of

Europe's "Christian roots." Around the world already this pagan regurgitation began a few years ago when magicians and sorcerers were legalized and esoteric cults and miracle healers were recognized. Today, however, in Germanic and Protestant northern Europe, ancient beliefs such as Wicca are making a comeback and, particularly in the Slavic world, old pagan agricultural festivals are returning revived somewhat too imaginatively in Ukraine and northern Russia. Even among the peoples of Central Asia after the breakup of the USSR, despite state atheism, Siberian and Central Asian peoples kept Buddhist or Muslim on the surface have rediscovered Buriat shamanism, for example, once again there arises a desire to return to the old ways of looking at the world without necessarily having to go through the mediation of traditional religions or ideologized political powers (as quasi-religions)

It should be warned that the word Russian, which one will encounter very often, does not have much bearing on a well-defined nationality, but denotes exclusively during the Middle Ages a Slavic (or assimilated) inhabitant of Russian lands and his language.

Let us add that the most current Russian word for paganism is *jazyc'estvo* translatable as *belonging to a certain people* in the sense that those who practice it do not belong to the "Christianized people," but to a different one. A meaning thus semantically much broader than *pagans* and not so negative. The Russian word is from the 11th cent. and refers back to the division of peoples recognizable through the different languages in the biblical legend of the tower of Babel and is therefore also a tacit witness to a multi-ethnic situation in the Russian land that the Christian powerhouse in Kyiv (and later that in Moscow) was not always able to deal with successfully, resigning itself to trying to keep urban culture (minimal, compared to massive urbanization in the Western Middle Ages) separate from peasant culture and thus condemning itself to have to endure the so-called dual-faith (*dvojeverje*) until the 19th cent. AD.

Then there is the inherent problem of being convinced that the concepts of god, religion, etc. elaborated over two thousand years of Christianity are absolute and unquestionable concepts and that any other ideas about the same "objects of discussion" are classified in a hostile way of inferior rank and always alien to us. Idolater, pagan, polytheist, animist, non-believer, etc. are all words often used with strong negativity and deflect any research on the subject.

In the past, many ambiguous terms were introduced by European ethnographers to distinguish dominant religions' self-styled bearers of universal truths and ethics from others scattered throughout the colonial world. Consequently, a term such as an *animism* (every object has a living and divine nature) ascribed most often to Nordic paganism and its mythology had a raison d'être exclusively in placing those beliefs on a lower rung to devalue them in the rich marketplace of ideas.

Why should mythology, *because it is pagan*, be ostracized as "superstition," a word that, while laden with negative meanings in almost all European languages, meant *religious practice existing beyond the rites permitted by the Roman imperial state*?

Myth and Mythology are words derived from Greek indicating moreover now an oral narrative is an organic collection of them. Mind you, however, while Greco-Roman paganism and its mythology were held in high esteem by Christian thought at least as the predecessors of "medieval knowledge" (*Saint Sophia*), for the Nordic peoples on this subject everything remains almost unknown.

To admit the existence of their *mythology* among these peoples at that time in history was impossible since they would be attributed to a civilization to which they were not yet entitled. Yet Christianity had sprung up and was flourishing at the expense of Greco-Roman civilization, entrenched and ancient with its *pagan state religion* as the foundation of power (Julius Caesar, for example, assumed the high sacred role of *Pontifex Maximus* in 63 B.C.). The rising church, however, within the power of the Empire imposed before anything else that the greatest space is left for the greatest god of all, the Christian god, and in addition, since the borders of the Empire for many more years remained Hadrian's Wall in England and in Central Europe the Rhine and 'Elbe basin, it ensured that the mythologies of the Slavic and Baltic (or steppe) peoples continued to be spoken of less and less.

The Romans had well-developed official mythology in a major *body of* literature that had been systematized for centuries. Their pre-Christian pantheon moreover was enriched with new gods whenever the Empire conquered a new region with its people, and, albeit rarely, the Romans noted some peculiarity of the religions of their subjects and respective gods. For example, Pliny the Elder or Tacitus (as mentioned earlier) write about the Germano-Baltic beliefs.

Be that as it may, clashes between Christian propaganda centers and pagan outbreaks were very frequent, although contemporary observers considered them second-order episodes. We could already start with Gregory the Great, who in the seventh century AD was one of the first to have first-hand news about the Slavs migrating south in correspondence with Maximus, bishop of Thessalonica[2]. Four centuries later, however, Christianity appears to be in retreat while the pagans have by no means disappeared. On the contrary, lustrated by the blessing with Christian holy water, they persevered undaunted in their religions and rites, sometimes in hiding. New expedients were therefore implemented by Rome (and Constantinople) to circumvent the problem of overly forced conversions and to somewhat dampen the mutual hatred Gregory the Great attempted to circumscribe ideological hostility with pagans by recommending not so much of fighting customs and traditions or destroying possible places of worship and eliminating them by force (despite everything, weapons were never banned), as much as integrating them into Christian customs and morals by possibly assimilating their festivals and rites under the protection of the saints venerated by the church (sometimes inventing new ones for the purpose). If one takes into account that Christianity was a "citizen religion" which at that time was at the height of success, that solution suggested then was the best growing since the new faith always involved subjection to secular powers sponsored by the church itself.

Neopaganism is, on the other hand, a spiritual movement that embraces a heterogeneous variety of new religious movements, inspired by a revival of ancient pagan spiritualities[7]. This movement developed mainly in the West during the second half of the twentieth century[8]. The

---

[7] James Lewis 2003, pp. 375 - 379
[8] Wouter Hanegraaff 1998, p. 278 ff.

religions included in the movement range from philosophies of life that appeal to continuity with past polytheistic religious experiences to entirely new, syncretic, and universalistic belief systems[9] defined by these characteristics as eclectic[10]. Although the worldview, theology, and the human being vary profoundly between one neopagan religion and another, there is a tacit sharing of a naturalistic and humanistic approach to existence[11]. Neopagan movements are often referred to as earth religiosity.

The term neopaganism is a neologism based on the term *paganism* popularized beginning in 1968 with the publication of the first issues of the *Green Egg*, a neopagan magazine run by the Church of All Worlds. The lemma is now quietly used by most neopagan communities to refer to Western post-Christian religions that can be included in the group in the same way as one identifies oneself as "Christian," "Jewish," or "Taoist"[12], although adherents of Gentile religions also called reconstructionist generally prefer the omission of the prefix *neo-*,[13] since they use the ancient rituals still found in the historical texts of the time: thus theirs would not be a modern reconstruction but reuse of ancient rituals.

Many neopagans recall as the ideal origin of their respective religious movements the speculations of many Renaissance intellectuals, who recovered, studied, and imitated the literary knowledge of Greco-Roman classicism. This cultural heritage was one of the main factors in the recovery of a humanist ideal of interest in and exaltation of man, ideally

---

[9] Michael York 2005, pp. 99 - 112

[10] Margot Adler 2006, pp. 457 - 471

[11] Salvatore Natoli 2007, pp. 183-185

[12] Margot Adler 2006, pp.342-345

[13] Isaac Bonewits 2006, pp. 192-197

opposed by them to the Christian-medieval conception of the human being, conceived as a mortifying man as such, being that he was accorded real value not as such but only in the perspective of his relationship with God. Many neopagans also recall the ideal origin of their respective religious movements speculations by many intellectuals of the heterogeneous Enlightenment movement, which was characterized by a harsh critique of the typical beliefs of the Abrahamic religions and by the desire to recover a supposed original natural religion, uniting all men as such, according to a typically cosmopolitan ideal.

The historical origin of neopaganism occurs in the 19th century with the emergence of Northern European Romanticism, which led to the spread of such phenomena as the Viking resurgence in the British Isles and Scandinavia and the Völkisch movement in Germany. The revival of Germanic religion stemmed from a heightened interest, typical of Romanticism and nineteenth-century nationalism. It was this climate that saw the formation of Ethene roots and Celticism in northwestern Europe. England represented one of the strongest epicenters of the pagan revival, which involved the appearance of the first Druidist groups and associations of an occult character such as the 'hermetic order of the Golden Dawn and the ordo templi orientis, which attempted to mix into their doctrine elements extrapolated from the Egyptian religion, the Jewish Kabbalah, and other traditions exotic. Influenced by James George Frazer's *The Golden Bough* several prominent writers and artists were involved in occult activity.

Neopaganism includes all those new religions that draw more or less directly on the pagan cults of 'ancient Europe. Religions such as Wicca, which is sometimes referred to as the *Old Religion* (an expression promulgated by Margaret Murray), or Fyrnsidu, whose name means "ancient tradition," are proposed as new spiritualities but bringing back to light the pre-Christian Weltanschauung, that is, that way of seeing the world that places human beings not above but within the system of nature. These concepts were rediscovered only in conjunction with the spread of the Enlightenment and humanistic philosophies. The human being is thus, in the various neopagan religions, paralleled by being regarded as the lord of his person, morals, and society, and a member of an eternal and cyclical universal equilibrium. Neopagan religions of the reconstructionist type appeal to a continuity that reconnects them with the ancient, although it is often recognized that contaminations and adaptation to certain modern views are inevitable. Wiccan religion itself, eclectic by definition, describes itself as a modern form of a hypothetical ancient monotheistic spirituality centered on the worship of the Mother Goddess and widespread in European areas during the Neolithic period.

In absolute terms, it is difficult to accurately quantify the number of Neopagans in the world. Although in countries such as the United States and Canada, where there are legally recognized neopagan churches and adherents are free to practice publicly and set up seminaries and temples, in several other nations many neopagans avoid making their membership in neopaganism public because of social conventions or environmental circumstances[14].

Furthermore, it is virtually impossible to establish a correlation between how many are publicly neopagan and

---

[14] Salvatore Natoli 2000, pp. 76-79

how many privately adhere to this belief[15]. Estimates based on objective data, such as the number of adherents who have publicly declared themselves as such and the number of sites referring to them, show that the tradition to be most widespread is the radically universalistic Wicca[16], which constitutes the most studied neo-pagan phenomenon and consequently the one on which it is easiest to make diffusion considerations. Some surveys conducted in the North American territory calculated the number of Neopagans ranging from 307,000[17] to 768,400, in a general confirmation of the worldwide million estimated by Adherents.com[18]

From Latin *paganus*, thus "villager," and later "pagan"; the change in meaning may be because the ancient religion endured longer in villages than in cities; according to another hypothesis *paganus*, which already had in classical Latin the meaning of "civilian, bourgeois, non-military," thus contrasting with *miles*, would have acquired the new meaning because the early Christians, who considered themselves militia of Christ, called infidels *pagans*, i.e., "bourgeois," it was then easy to label as pagans those who did not join the church army, *'qui in militia nonascribebantur'*[19]. More recently it has been argued that the *pagus* was an entity not only social but also religious, with its sacred public

---

[15] See Morgan Ravenwood 2006, online article: Hate Crimes And Hate Incidents: Shedding New Light On Pagan Persecution.

[16] Michael York, 2005 pp. 163-164

[17] The Graduate Center - American Religious Identification Survey: including 134,000 Wiccans, 33,000 Celticists, and 140,000 other Neopagans

[18] Religions by Adherents, from adherents.com. Estimates updated to 2005

[19] Domenico and Carlo Magri 2011, pp. 73-77

festivals (*paganalia*), so that *pagans* would be the ones who kept faithful to the traditional sacred values of the *pages*.

A second term by which pagans were named, this time specifically referring to the great people who remained such while living in the cities, is *gentiles*, a word of Latin origin (*gentiles*, from *gens*, i.e., *people*), roughly mirroring the Greek *ethnicoi*, which in turn was used in Hellenistic circles as a translation of a word common among Jews, *goim, which stood* for all those who were not part of the Jewish community either by ethnicity or religion. This name thus labeled all people belonging to *a people*, taking on ethnological meanings.

Today the names *gentiles, gentilitas,* and *gentilism* are used, deprived of their ethnic meanings, to refer to that branch of modern Paganism that tends to refer as faithfully as possible to the ancient pre-Christian pagan religions, using the original ritualism that has come down to the present day, as opposed to the so-called heterodox pagans, who do not refer to any particular ancient tradition but base their worship according to more recent rituals and religious types. The term *pagans* probably arose as a disparaging function against those who adhered to traditional religions, referred to as *pagan* dwellers, more backward than the inhabitants of large cities. After the establishment of Christianity in the 'Roman Empire, the remaining followers of the ancient religion had gathered in the countryside away from the city life that had by then become pro-Christian. The so-called *pagans* were thus originally the people who, living in the *pages*, tended to maintain a rather rural lifestyle, as well as not coming into contact with the cultural and political developments of the state.

The name then immediately took on a derogatory connotation, soon becoming an insult indicating uncouth and ignorant people.

With the advent of Christianity as the state religion, the term began to be used by Christians to refer to all those who refused to convert, lumping them in with the *pagan* inhabitants who, being isolated, tended to keep their original religious traditions alive. All this would lead, then, the Christians of the time to equate the idea of 'campy' with that of 'non-Christian': '*Ex locorum agrestium compitis et pagis pagani vocantur*[20]'.

Another explanation, proposed by Christine Mohrmann, would explain the translation according to the thesis that the term paganus was used simply to denote any *outsider*, that is, a person who stood outside a certain community or group of people. According to this thesis, therefore, the meanings of 'country dweller' and 'civilian' would be nothing more than mere specializations.

Christians of the time would only create a further specialization of the term, placing as a group precisely the community of believers in Christ; those who remained outside were *outsiders*, pagans: '*qui alieni a civitate Dei ex locorum agrestium conpitis et pagis pagani vocantur*[21]'

The term was later used to describe all non-Christian religions, including Judaism and Islam: it thus took on the meaning of *non-Christian*, just as *barbarian* indicated *non-Roman*. With the Renaissance and modern eras, the term *pagans* abandoned any negative meaning and began to be

---

[20] Paulus Orosius 1849, pp. 377-382
[21] Paulus Orosius 1849, pp. 382- 384

generally used to indicate, again narrowing its scope, only the ancient religions practiced in 'pre-Christian Europe and, by extension, also those of the pre-Columbian Judaic civilizations.

Paganism originated in ancient times, probably arising from the combination of several animistic cults native to Europe and America with a theological system that spread with the parallel expansion of populations of Indo-European stock. Its evolution then proceeded over the centuries to form what was the theology-, cosmology-, and philosophy-based religiosity of the great civilizations of the past. Pagan religions contributed profoundly to the formation of the cultures of peoples, who tended to recount through elaborate allegorical mythologies those mysteries about the divine to which often only the priestly orders were deeply initiated. Mythologies are fables, and metaphors that served to explain high and sublime concepts to the uncouth peoples; deep theological knowledge was always hidden behind the mythological zest. Paganism was distinguished into a series of traditions, which were strongly linked to the culture of the people who conceived them: pagan religions offered multiple viewpoints encoding the same meaning, so anyone had the opportunity to practice even two traditions simultaneously, praying to and invoking Zeus and parallel Isis.

In its spread, Christianity, slowly destroyed paganism from within, crushing its ideologies (depriving myths of their esoteric meaning for example) and simultaneously physically demolishing it through the destruction of sacred places and philosophical academies rather than the physical elimination of worshippers, priests, and intellectuals. Ideological repression was enacted not only through the emptying of theologies, but also through the conversion of symbols, very folkloric figures, and widely well-liked deities and therefore by misleading their meaning, from mystical-religious to maleficent. Only Emperor Julian, the last pagan ruler, attempted a restoration of the old religion, organizing it similarly to Christianity, with a central church and a universalistic attitude, as well as calling it *Hellenism*, since Paganism had never had an official name until that time. In the 18th century, the new philosophers (notably Voltaire) described it as a champion of "enlightenment" against Christian obscurantism and as a champion of freedom against the absolutism of the lower empire. During Romanticism, too, people were passionate about the character, seeing him as a Romantic ante litteram, a lucid and desperate spirit. Julian was an enlightened character; his reign was marked by complete tolerance toward any religious denomination and intransigence toward the church's abuse of power and the fanaticism of the Christian faithful[22]. Originally a Christian, Julian converted to paganism and proceeded to make a desperate attempt to rescue the religion of his ancestors, although it had long since been unhinged and in the process of collapse. Julian devoted his entire life to the pagan cause; he also produced several works in which, like most intellectuals of the time, he accused Christianity of arrogance, closure, and irrationality, as opposed to a pagan religion characterized by an ideological openness that did not impose itself on the populace by obscuring its rational capacities. Julian also proceeded to support other religions, such as 'Judaism, which had also been harmed (albeit to a lesser degree) by Christian

---

[22] On June 17, 362 Julian issued an edict, succinctly called the edict of toleration

impetuosity: he ordered, for example, the rebuilding of the long-destroyed temple in Jerusalem, although this project of his had no positive outcome. In general, the emperor's attempt was unsuccessful, primarily because of the brevity of his reign, after the end of which paganism proceeded in its inexorable decline. In 393 Emperor Theodosius, I officially declared the illegality of Paganism throughout the empire and permanently closed the last remaining temples in operation; the death penalty explicitly became the sentence reserved for those who refused conversion to Christianity. Paganism remained latent until the modern era especially in Europe, while it remained the principal faith in Asia and Africa. In Asia, the attempt to eradicate paganism is still ongoing today, so much so that the Indian peoples of Orissa respond to Christian proselytizing, the only faith to pursue religious proselytizing, by driving Christians and prelates from their lands.

But what was the common thread, which linked all pre-Christian peoples? in general, one can speak of "polytheism" related mainly to nature and the environment that housed these rural populations. Part of this "cult" then were various elements such as the seasons, the weather, and the animals themselves. In short, a way of life that was less barbaric, than the official religions wanted to portray. There was therefore no single vengeful god, but a set of "forces" generating everything. Those who look to paganism for answers about the origin of life, and its meaning, are unlikely to find them, just as it is impossible to find them in any monotheistic religion that exists today.

Religions were created by man, which is precisely why he cannot explain what he occurred before him with them. The attitude of a *paganus* in pre-Christian rural villages was very simple. To live off the fruit of one's labor, offered by mother earth, to ingratiate oneself with the gods who could make a harvest or sowing successful. A close relationship in short with the land, a huge bond with one's people and ethnicity, defended to the last from Christian invasion. All too obvious to make a comparison, today, between man/environment and obvious the conclusions that can be drawn.

Man today does not make the land fruitful but exploits it as anything that can be useful to him to procure money. There are also those who today define with extreme superficiality a pagan as an atheist, nothing could be more wrong, while not having a single God in whom to believe and obey, the pagan certainly believes, but he believes above all in what is in front of him, what gives him benefit he believes in the fruits he feeds on, in the land he cultivates, in the rain that makes it proliferate. This is where the "loyalty to the land" of the pre-Christian peoples comes from. With extreme naivety and purity, they can understand that there is something benevolent in what surrounds them, they do not see the god of the monotheists, but they see, the winds, the seas, the mountains, and the sky, this is their faith and to this, they dedicate their religiosity and spirituality.

Paganism denies creative omnipotence and divine providence, in a world ruled by fate. For Christianity, on the other hand, history is in the hands of God, the omnipotent creator of the world whose care he takes, leading humanity, through mysterious ways, to the end, he has assigned to it; but because he has created man free, he may not correspond to God's plan, turn against him, and then God - pulls from every evil a good, that is, he succeeds in making even man's negative sides contribute to the end of creation and history. History, therefore, is all of God as the first and main cause and all of the men as the second and instrumental cause. Paganism or ancient Greece and Rome, have an analogous role (where similarity is less than similarity) to the A. T. than to the N. T., they had to prepare Christian Rome, as Mosaism had to prepare the Gospel; pagan Rome is not absolute evil, which does not exist since it is deprivation of good, but it is an ontologically good entity, though accompanied by the religious-moral disorder of paganism. In contrast, Mosaism was good in itself, but imperfect and was perfected by Christ. Rome dies pagan so that it may rise again as a Christian.[23]. Paganism is the absence of supernatural order so that the acquired virtues of the pagans cannot be said to be perfect, but neither can it be said (as Bajo did) that they are sinful in themselves, they can be perfected by the grace of Christ that makes them supernatural, orders them to their one true ultimate end. Paganism submits virtue not to God the creator but to idols or gods, which obscure the intellect, divert the will and pervert human capacities. The actions, in themselves naturally good of the pagans, aimed at honors, glory, and earthly fame, it must be admitted that these acquired natural virtues, though not ordered to the ultimate end and having no supernatural value, enabled the ancient Greeks and Romans to overcome some unruly passions and to attain a high degree of culture, order, and discipline, individual and social.

The history of the world has two capitals and two religions, the Holy Trinity which has its headquarters in the Rome of the Popes; and the counter church of Satan which has two main headquarters: the deicide Jerusalem destroyed by Titus and the Rome of the Caesars, invaded by the barbarians,

---

[23] Cf. Barnard Lesile W. 1990, p. 79.

which became the Christian Rome with Constantine (4th century) but returned under the influence of paganism with Humanism and the Renaissance (15th-16th centuries). Paganism was characterized by pantheistic polytheism and polytheistic idolatry.

Let us now analyze the different pagan and Christian conceptions of the state a) Paganism:

his political conception is naturalist, that is, the ultimate term of man and society is earthly existence and visible things, there is nothing beyond and above the state, it is a kind of pan-statism that absorbs the individual totally (totalitarianism). State and religion are one, indeed religion is at the service of the state, it is an *instrumentum regni*. Moreover, "Greco-Roman pagan religion had neither dogma nor morality derived from it and was naturalistic itself, its gods were not transcendent and personal entities, but mythologized human beings." The ancient pagans knew neither private and individual freedom nor educational or family freedom.

(b) Christianity

Christianity brought two new ideas that paganism lacked: the transcendence of the personal God and divine providence.

1) Divine transcendence:

God is essentially distinct from the world and man, any confusion about pantheism was eradicated. Moreover, Christianity was not the religion of one tribe, one city, or one people, it is a universal religion, that respects different mentalities, cultures, ways of life, and local traditions, where they do not contain elements contrary to sound reason to dogma and morality.

The state ceased to be an absolute and totalizing deity, to become the union of several men given an end under an authority that would procure the common temporal welfare of the community, on pain of losing authority by becoming a tyranny. Furthermore, since what is earthly and temporal - by the hierarchy of ends - is inferior to what is heavenly and spiritual, the state must be subservient to the church, as the body to the soul, and help it - through good legislation that makes possible a moral life already on this earth - to lead souls to heaven.

2) Providence:

If God is personal and infinitely transcends every creature (even angelic ones), nevertheless He is the creator and being infinite Goodness, He takes care of His creatures, the irrational ones are directed by physical laws (the sun rises and sets every day...) and the rational ones lead them by the hand, day by day, step by step, to their supernatural end, respecting their freedom.

The state is a creature of God; in fact, man is a social animal by nature, and therefore owes it honor and glory like all other creatures; in particular, it must be subordinate to the spiritual power-the Church-which God has established on earth for the supernatural common welfare of men. Thus ceases every form of pagan statuary, Caesarism, pan-statism, or political totalitarianism, which reappears when man and nations turn away from Christ and his Church. In paganism, the basis is omnipotent creation and divine providence in a world governed by fate.

For Christianity, on the other hand, history is in the hands of God, the almighty creator of the world whose care he takes, leading humanity, through mysterious ways, to the end he has assigned to it; but because he has created man free, he may not correspond to God's plan, turn against him, and then God, with his infinite omnipotence and wisdom, pulls out of every evil a good, that is, he can make even the negative sides of man contribute to the end of creation and history.

History, therefore, is all of God as the first and principal cause and all of the men as the second and instrumental cause. The keystone of history (as St. John's *Revelation* and St. Augustine's *City of God* teach) is Christ the redeemer and judge who helps his elect or the "city of God" to triumph against the wicked and Satan's supposes (who for the sake of self despise God). If pagan Rome falls in 410 at the hands of Alaric barbarians, it is because the Rome of the Caesars is not the center of the world, rather it is the one that persecutes Christ in its martyrs and must give way to the Rome of the Popes. The prevalence of Christianity in the Greco-Roman world determined a new direction in philosophy. Christianity never and still does not present itself as a philosophy; it is not an adherence to a new doctrine, but an encounter with Christ that revolutionizes life.

However, Christianity could not have established itself permanently over the highest philosophical expressions of pagan culture if it had not done, in addition to the simple work of proselytism, a high-level work of doctrinal clarification, capable of defining the Christian worldview and related theological problems: to do this, philosophical thinking became indispensable. Moreover, the reflection of Christian thinkers was stimulated by the urgent need to defend themselves against the accusations of their opponents, Jews, and pagans. Jews and pagans to prevent the spread of Christianity formulated precise accusations against it[24].

Christianity was immediately blamed by the pagans for producing a softening of the empire's solid moral foundations that would expose the empire to the penetrations of the barbarians: on the one hand, Christianity had created a set of values antithetical to those of the pagans; on the other hand, and for the most part, the reason for the empire's downfall lay in its basic political fragility.

To protect the Church from accusations of provoking the dissolution of Roman civilization, Augustine had wanted to explain that the Empire had indeed, up to a certain point, had the function of reuniting and subsuming under one authority all the peoples first dispersed, but now found the reasons for its decadence in the supreme will of God, according to which it will be the Church, from now on, that will guide men toward the only possible salvation, that represented by faith.

Its decadence could not, therefore, be blamed in any way on the Christian religion, but was the result of a historical process teleologically preordained by God in the function of the resurrection of those men who, by living in God's mercy and avoiding losing their freedom in yielding to evil temptations, would be able to enjoy divine salvation when the city of men was destroyed forever. In this sense, the

---

[24] Jewish accusations: in the Talmud (Hebrew term for post-Biblical doctrines and writings put in writing around the 5th century CE) and post-Talmudic literature Jesus is called Notzri of the Nazarene, other times called Ben Pandera, at other times Ben Stada (Ben = born of): in the former case with allusion to the father, in the latter about the mother who was allegedly cast out by her husband Joseph because she was suspected of adultery (strada = adulteress) with a Roman soldier named Pandera.

decadence of Rome was interpreted as a herald of this coming destruction and, therefore, as an exhortation for men to abandon their attachment to earthly things and turn to the only Good represented by God; it was an interpretation that continued throughout the Middle Ages, especially following the struggles for supremacy between the Pope and the Holy Roman Empire.

St. Paul recalls how the Godhead was incarnated in Christ: Christianity worships God in man. To worship God in man is to worship man as God. Jews and Muslims, on the other hand, are opposed to this idea. If I worship God in reason I worship God as a rational being, so I worship reason. If I worship God in the man I worship man himself. If I diminish God in the man I effectively suppress his difference from man. Even if a man is the garment of God, one does not transcend the human being. Behind a God who has his image in man can conceal no content other than the human being[25].

If Christianity is the self-divinization of man, how does it differ from paganism? The 20 Jewish accusations: in the Talmud (Hebrew term for post-Biblical doctrines and writings put in writing around the 5th century CE) and post-Talmudic literature Jesus is called Notzri of the Nazarene, other times called Ben Pandera, at other times Ben Stada (Ben = born of): in the former case with allusion to the father, in the latter about the mother who was allegedly cast out by her husband Joseph because she was suspected of adultery (strada = adulteress) with a Roman soldier named Pandera.

Paganism worships qualities, Christianity the essence of man. Paganism does not deify man as man, but man as a

---

[25] Pier Franco Beatrice 1990, pp. 7-14

great artist, emperor, etc., also as a man but only by accident. The pagan is therefore idolatrous because he does not rise to the essence of man as such, but deifies certain images of him, certain properties, and individualities. He is polytheistic because the properties he chants are of many men. Christianity is monotheistic because the essence of man is one. The pagan has sexed and national gods, but before the Christian God all are equal. This God is man, with absolute identity and indifference to all differences and oppositions. By deifying men the pagan proves that for him man is not God and that he wants rather to make man God, but he cannot because he starts with the man.

Christianity does not deify anyone; man's divinity is taken for granted by it. Men inherit the nobility of divinity from their father, man. In paganism, they win it by merit. Christian humility versus pagan pride. The more a man is in his essence (Christian) the less he is in imagination (in the pagan, imagination replaces lack of reality).

The pagan is made God, by consultation or own decision, while the Christian is born God. In short, pagans deified man only in an illusory and superficial way, Christians completely and radically. In paganism, divinity is a privilege, and in Christianity a legitimate common good. Christ is the end of all deification of man because he is God for all (pagans deified men because their gods already had human characters).

Paganism is a religion, indeed a religiosity, a religious attitude, founded on what-if we want to use Nietzsche's 'expression-we might call fidelity to the earth, to the finite. It is a form of religiosity whose paradigm remains the natural one, it is a religiosity that speaks to us of birth and death, that speaks to us of a great cycle, that speaks to us of a living reality, that embodies the forces of nature. In short, nature is the backdrop against which these great tales, which are the mythological tales, stand out. In this sense, one can speak of fidelity to the earth. More exactly still it would be the case to speak of fidelity to nature, but to an animated nature, because this is first and foremost paganism. Paganism responds to this idea: that nature is alive, that nature has its dynamic, its soul, its reality that must be respected, and that above all speaks to us. It speaks to us in riddles, it speaks to us by throwing messages at us, and it speaks to us by telling us something that we must listen to and interpret.

Respect for nature: not only respect for nature but also an awareness that nature is also passable, it is like a horizon, it is a backdrop against which the stories stand out in which we decipher the signs that tell us about our deepest realities. Precisely, nature must be respected and listened to because it is alive, indeed it is life, it is our life, and it is the very origin of life. And, like life, all its expressions are themselves animated. Deities are nothing but forms of nature itself, expressions of this life force that has its place in nature.

So fidelity to the earth, respect and listening to nature, nature as the ultimate limit, religion, which, precisely binds us in this ultimate sense of finiteness. Nature is the work of God. It comes out of God's hands and God judges it as his product, and he judges it as his good product. "Valde bonum," "strongly good," is what comes out of the hands, the hands of God. But, precisely, it comes out of God's hands, it is something to which God gives a kind of start, then letting it take its course, withdrawing to Himself. This idea of God withdrawing who, wanting to let nature be, must, in some way, withdraw and retreat is a Jewish idea, but later picked up by the Christian tradition as well.

God is the creator of nature, but precisely insofar as He is the creator, nature has its freedom, its independence vis-à-vis God Himself, which sinks into its absolute transcendence concerning nature itself. Right here we encounter a principle that will justify within the tradition Christian, that which is the recognition of the possibility of transcending the limits of nature. Nature is not something ultimate, nature is not the horizon within which experience is possible and beyond which there is nothing, there is nothing because God if he is something, divinity if it is something is not except to the extent that it is embodied in nature. Nature, we have seen, for the Christian is the scene of his life, it is the field on which his life is played out. But the decisive principle of his own life is elsewhere, it refers back to that elsewhere which is God, which is God himself. The principle, as he would have said Kierlegaard, of freedom. While the pagan in nature sees it as an also passable horizon of his experience, the Christian is originally called to go beyond this same horizon in the name of that freedom whose foundation is God's retraction, the fact that God created nature has retracted himself to himself and let nature be in its freedom. From this point of view, we cannot properly speak of fidelity to the earth or fidelity to nature on the part of the Christian. The Christian is faithful to something else and different, he is faithful not so much to nature and the earth, but something other than nature and the earth.

To the spirit. Of course, here the discussion becomes particularly complex and vast, but when we say that the Christian is not faithful to the earth, but faithful to the spirit, we are saying that the Christian, unlike the pagan, is a free man, that is, a man who is responsible for his actions. Not that the pagan is not, but he is different. There is an identification for the pagan with the natural reality within which he lives, there is a kind of immediacy. "Eros," for example, someone said is a typically Christian thing. It would seem strange to me because Christianity if it ever censors erotic experience, censors an experience that instead the pagan lived as absolutely natural. But precisely because the pagan lived this experience as absolutely natural, it made no problem for him. To the Christian, on the other hand, deferring as the ultimate principle of his experience to otherness, to another than nature, the properly natural elements, including "eros," do pose a problem. The Christian is said to have posited "eros" by excluding it. The well-known dialectical mechanism, but consists precisely in referring back to a spiritual principle of a higher order. What is this spiritual principle of a higher order embodied in God? It is freedom, that is, responsibility for all one's actions. The Christian cannot repair himself within his belonging to nature. Nature does not more the safeguarding of the Christian, the justification of the Christian, because justification is beyond. So not fidelity to the earth, but fidelity to the spirit.

Christianity moves us out of a mythological world, such as the typically pagan world was, and into a world that is instead historical, a world of realities that are no longer purely fantasized, or imagined, but of realities that want to be realities, historical realities. And why this? Because of animate nature, nature expresses itself in the form of deities who are nothing but forces of nature, who are indeed nothing but nature in its infinite manifestations, here this world can have no other vehicle, no other way of expressing itself than a myth.

For what is a myth if not living nature in its becoming, in its infinite metamorphosis? What are mythic tales, these mythic tales that germinate, that come forth as if from an inexhaustible bottom, precisely the bottom of nature? What are these mythical tales if not nature itself in its performing, in its showing itself, in its speaking to the man who lives in symbiosis with it?

The mythological world is this, but if the mythological world is this, Christianity comes out of myth, it comes out of myth and distances itself from nature, it no longer lives in symbiosis with nature, nature no longer speaks to him as if it were that living reality in which man participates and with which man identifies. Rather, nature is the scene of his life, the field of action; it is what gives him the tools to build, precisely, a world that is no longer mythical, but historical. Building.

Everything that Christianity subsequently produced can be understood only from this consideration. It is also true that we could also turn this argument around and recognize that the opposition presupposes entanglements and obscure solidarity between Christianity and paganism. For while it is true that paganism is the religion of the earth, of nature, of myth while the Christianity is the religion of the spirit, of the transcendence of God and thus of a radically historical hope, it is also true that there are in Christianity many pagan elements and there are in paganism anticipations of elements, which Christianity would later adopt, develop and make it's own.

Christianity then, or rather, the Christian tradition used the categories elaborated in the pagan sphere, the philosophical categories elaborated in the pagan sphere. This is true not only of the later tradition, the scholastic tradition for example, but one might ask whether the Creed of Nicaea, this founding act of Christian dogmatics, would be thinkable if we bracketed those pagan categories that were used by the Church Fathers and then not only by the Church Fathers but also by the doctors of the Church. But beyond the Fathers and the doctors, there is the immense reality of mysticism. Well within Christian mysticism, we encounter experiences whose roots certainly are pre-Christian, they go beyond Christianity itself. From this point of view what strikes us is dark, deep solidarity between two perspectives on the world that, as we have seen, are antagonistic and fundamentally different.

But then, again, let us bring the discussion back to the philosophical problem we encounter here. The philosophical problem is indeed all that of a definition of what is proper to paganism and what is proper to Christianity, so much so that on several occasions we see attempts, precisely attempts carried out philosophically to take up again, to reactivate, to re-actualize, to put back into circulation visions, images of the world of pagan type or attempts to find authentic Christianity beyond these admixtures.

The first three centuries of the Christian era were marked by severe persecutions by paganism against Christianity; however, any generalization is incorrect, either one that made the three centuries continuous persecution or one that tends to minimize the extent of the persecutions. The confrontation was, after all, necessary, given the opposition between Christianity and pagan Panstatism.

The first occasion of confrontation between the Roman Empire and Christianity was the trial of Jesus[26]. In recent decades, some scholars have attempted to overturn the setting given to the trial by the Gospels, attributing the initiative of the trial itself to the Roman power and not to the Jewish authority. From a scholarly point of view, the arguments of these scholars have proved to be very flimsy and easy to refute. For the Gospels, the initiative was from the Jews, even though the execution was from the Romans. All four accounts in the Gospels show the decisive responsibility of the Jews and reduce the part Pilate had in Jesus' death to his yielding, against will, to the urgings of the high priests and the crowd. According to the distinguished scholar of Greco-Roman history, the clash between the Roman Empire and Christianity was first and foremost a religious clash, Christianity was persecuted as a religion, and Rome's conversion to Christ was largely brought about by the approach of many, disgusted with the corruption of the present, to a religion that involved a stern moral commitment and the austere practice of personal and familial virtues. Sordi writes that the conversion of the pagan world to Christianity was first and foremost a religious conversion and that the immense power of attraction that the new faith exerted from the beginning, in the greatest ancient empire and its cosmopolitan capital, was revealed by its ability to respond to the deepest religious needs of the human soul, which were also, at the particular historical moment when Christianity entered the world, the religious needs of the Roman world."

---

[26] Marta Sordi 2004, pp. 117-124

Christianity knew how to answer the passionate questions that men were asking and particularly the ancient Romans and conquered the ancient world. Christianity was not a revolutionary, pacifist, or subversive phenomenon; it accepted the state and Caesar as "established in power by our God"[27] but could not admit imperial worship as if it were a deity; it obeyed and fought for Rome as a political power established by God "from whom descends all power," but refused to offer incense to the gods and Emperor *divus Caesar*.

There was, however, a kind of prolonged pagan resistance, against Christianity, carried on by a small intellectual aristocracy very much attached to the pristine Greco-Roman traditions, which acted in the name of a tolerance that the Christians did not have (Proclus, Simmachus, Julian the Apostate, Porphyry) of which today Alain de Benoist makes himself the herald and continuator.

In the three centuries between Christianity's entry into the empire and Constantine's conversion, the relationship between Christians and imperial power appears complexly articulated. Any generalization is incorrect: either the outdated one that made the three centuries of continuous persecution; or the one that tends to minimize the extent of the persecutions, even eliminating some of them, such as that of Domitian.

The persecution was made legally possible by a senate consultation in A.D. 35, by which the Senate, the body responds in the Julio-Claudian age for accepting or rejecting cults new to the empire, had rejected a proposal by Tiberius (14-37), who was interested in the pacification of Judea, to

---

[27] Tertullian, Apologetics 33:1.

recognize the lawfulness of the cult of Christ, removing it from the control of the Sanhedrin. The persecution did not begin until after 62. Nero (54-68) was the first to enforce the senate consult that proclaimed Christianity *superstition illicita* and ruthlessly persecuted the Christians of Rome, indicting them for the fire of 64[28]. After Nero, only Domitian (81-96), determined as he was to impose imperial worship, persecuted Christians, who were also present in the Roman aristocracy. Under Nero, as under Domitian, Christians were targeted in the same years as the Stoics, who still constituted Rome's best ruling class and opposed the theocratic transformation of the principate. Nerva (96-98) put an end to the persecution, but Trajan (98-117) could not repeat his veto, as Tiberius had already done, of accusations of Christianity, because he realized that public opinion, in the senate as well as in the popular masses, was hostile. Although the imperial cult was no longer imposed and was often used against Christians only as a pretext for accusing them of failing in their loyalty to the empire, especially in the eastern provinces, the rejection by the Christians themselves of the worship of all the gods of the empire, without the cover of a licit cult such as the Judaic religion had had since the time of Caesar, exposed them to the accusation of atheism and all the dark or infamous faults (the *flagitia mentioned by* Tacitus) that the popular mentality attributed to atheists. Thus, throughout the second century, from Trajan[29] to Marcus Aurelius (161-180), the emperors, convinced of the non-dangerousness of Christianity politically, sought to limit persecution by containing it within the extremely generic

---

[28] Tacitus, Ann XV, 44

[29] Of which we have the first official document: the rescript to Pliny then governor of Bithynia

confines of the senate-consultation (*Non licet esse Christianos*) of individual guilt of a religious character, deliberately ignoring Christianity as a Church (the mention of which would have resulted in condemnation as *collegium illicitum*) and strictly forbidding ex officio research: Christians could be charged only based on private, non-anonymous complaints and were virtually encouraged to go underground.

This situation of compromise, contested by intransigent pagans, who demanded a search by the state, and by Christians who noted its contradictions (and who began in this period, with apologia addressed to the emperors, to demand its correction) continued until Marcus Aurelius, when the spread among Christians of the Montanist heresy, with its anti-Roman attitudes and its provocations against the temples and statues of the gods, seeking martyrdom, induced the emperor to circumvent Trajan's ban on searching for Christians, allowing the office search of *sacrileges*, to whom public opinion equated Christians.

The prompt reaction of the Great Church, with its numerous apologia in the 70s of the 2nd century (Athenagoras, Meliton, Apollinaris) and its clear distancing from Montanist fanaticism, induced Marcus Aurelius, in the last years of his reign, to seek a solution: on the one hand, he demanded Christians to come out of hiding (which, moreover, they had not chosen) and manifest the loyalism they professed toward the state by open cooperation; on the other hand, he threatened Christians' accusers with the death penalty. Christianity remained *superstitio illicita*, but Christians were not sought as such: if they denounced and confessed, they were put to death, but their accuser was also condemned. What happened, precisely, under Commodus (180-1 92), son of Marcus Aurelius, to the accuser of the Christian senator Apollonius. This allowed the Church to come out of hiding, allowed Christian aristocrats to hold public office and serve the state, and discouraged private accusations. If Christians were deemed dangerous to public order, the charge of sacrilege allowed for ex officio searches.

Under Commodus and then under the Severans, the Church came out of hiding and claimed ownership of places of worship, assembly, and cemeteries, which until then had remained under the protection of private property: de-facto toleration was established, which did not prevent local persecution by governors of personally hostile provinces or coerced by mobs but excluded general persecution.

With Septimius Severus (193-211) the *collegia religionis causa*, which need no official recognition, allowed the Church to lawfully carry out its activities; so much so that, with Alexander Severus (222-235), the emperor himself, arbitrator of a dispute between the Church of Rome and a professional corporation, could openly judge in favor of the former[30].

The ecclesiastical organization is well known and looked up to. while the catechetical school of Alexandria, the first "Christian university," arouses esteem and interest even among pagans. Emperors and empresses are no longer given apologia, but treatises on theology: the integration of Christians in the empire is well underway, and with Philip the Arab (244-249) we have perhaps the first Christian emperor. The reaction comes with Decius (249-251) who, without naming the Christians, imposes by edict on all citizens of the empire the sacrifice to the gods and the

---

[30] Jacques Moreau 1977, pp. 89-92

withdrawal of a certificate (libellus) to attest to the sacrifice: for the Christians, made more sluggish by a long period of peace, it is the time of defections.

But the mass of the *lapsi* (Christians who, under threat, did not declare their faith) who, on the strength of the immunity they had obtained, again demanded admission to the Church, reveals the very strong vitality of Christianity and the futility of persecution conducted on the exclusively religious line of the old senate-consult. The enemies of the Christians realize that if Christianity is to be beaten, it must be fought as a Church: with Valerian (253-ca 260), in 257, the line of Trajan was abandoned for the first time, and members of the clergy and laymen of the ruling classes were struck down with a series of edicts, places of worship and burial were confiscated, and bloody general persecution was unleashed. When Gallienus (253-260: reigned with his father), son of Valerian, in 260 wished to restore peace in the empire, after his father had been defeated by the Persians, he could not merely tacitly cease persecutory measures but had to issue The first edict of toleration. With Gallienus Christianity became *religio licita*, confiscated church property was returned to the Church (Eusebius *H.E.* VII,13), and Christians in the ruling class engaged in public life and the army were explicitly exempted from the duty of sacrifice to the gods. There followed 40 years of peace, which would be interrupted by the terrible persecution of Diocletian (A.D. 303), which – was suspended in the West after the resignation of Maximian (305) and in the empire by Galerius' Edict of Serdica (311) - would find its true conclusion in the conversion of Constantine and the so-called Edict of Milan.

The unfolding of the persecutions, alternating with long periods of peace and cordial relations, reveals the falsity of the idea, which goes back to Zosimus and is taken up by Gibbon, of Christianity being present in the empire as a foreign, hostile body, the primary cause of its dissolution. On the contrary, Christianity was seen by the empire as a danger only at particular, circumscribed moments. For its part, Christian thought was never hostile, with rare exceptions, to the empire of Rome. The Christian loyalism toward Rome has its authoritative foundation, long before in the Apologists-from Justin to Meliton, from Athenagoras to Tertullian himself not yet a Montanist-in the apostolic letters: in chapter 13 of Paul's letter to the Romans and the First Petri (2:13 ff.). This is not an attitude of convenience, adopted to avoid the rigors of persecution, but the ability to distinguish with acute discernment what in the empire stems from the faults of men and pagan religion and what is, instead, the great ecumenical idea of Rome, the overcoming in a synthesis of law and a fundamentally peaceful civil order, of the ethnic differences between peoples, the recomposition of the antinomies between Greek and barbarian, the agreement between *imperium* and *pax*, which Seneca (*De Prov.* IV,1 4) expresses in the concept of pax Romana, understood as the inhabited and civilized world to which the empire ensures peace.

This Christian idea of empire, which is not post-Constantinian but even coexists with persecution, allows Athenagoras in 177 to express[31] a fervent wish for the enlargement of the empire and induces Tertullian, not yet a Montanist, to state that Christians pray to obtain from God *imperium securum, exercitus fortes, orbem quietum*[32], and rebut

---

[31] Athenagoras, chapter 37 of his supplication. Cf. Athenagoras. The Supplication for Christians. On the Resurrection of the Dead, in Corona Patrum Salesiana, XV, Turin 1947 edited by P. Ubaldi and M. Pellegrino
[32] Apol. 30,4

the accusations spread by opponents but not received by emperors, declaring[33]: *noster est magis Caesar a nostro Deo constitutus.*

"The Jews ask for a sign and the Greeks seek wisdom, but we preach Christ crucified, who scandal to the Jews and folly to the Greeks." With these words opens the first letter to the Corinthians[34] by the apostle Paul, who seems to grasp early on the wisdom-foolishness dialectic that will be the hallmark of the anti-Christian polemic. Indeed, paganism deploys its best minds to demonstrate how the figure of Jesus and the Christian proclamation falls into the category of unreasonableness. It is especially from the fourth century onward that the now triumphant Christianity would overthrow on paganism the very accusations of which it had been the object. During the second century, anti-Christian criticisms mostly fell within the framework of popular prejudices, unnecessarily cloaked in a veneer of plausibility: in the course of their meetings, Christians engage in anthropophagy and incest, worship a donkey's head, bow before the genitals of their priests, cause natural disasters, and perform spells of all sorts. These accusations, which often resulted in acts of open hostility, are answered by the exponents of the so-called early Latin apologetics, Tertullian and Minucius Felix, who show that the accusations made were the result of ignorance and malevolence.

From the third century on, the situation changes. Although prejudices continue to find wide credence in less educated circles, it is the intellectuals, especially Neoplatonic philosophers, custodians of the most authentic values of the

---

[33] Apol. 33,1
[34] Letter to the Corinthians (1:22-23)

great Hellenistic-Roman tradition of thought, who take on the "task" of demonstrating the absurdity of the Christian movement and its theological system. They grasped very well the danger posed by Christians, who, by refusing to adhere to the imperial cult, with all that it entailed, ended up introducing a disruptive and antisocial element into the socio-political structure. Among the various voices involved in the controversy, the most significant are those of Celsus and Porphyry.

The Celsus author of the *Alethès logos* ("Truthful Discourse") would probably have remained in the oblivion of history if the great Greek apologist Origen had not written a *Contra Celsum* thanks to which it is possible to reconstruct the gist of the accusations made by this philosopher who lived in the second half of the second century.

Celsus' work is important because, leaving aside the trite paraphernalia of petty and somewhat gossipy polemics, he seeks to dismantle the Christian message from within, with solid arguments. The starting point of his argument is that only a secular tradition constitutes the foundation and veracity (alethès) of all philosophical and theological discourse (logos). If only that which is ancient is endowed with value, what antiquity can Christianity exhibit? On what tradition is it founded? Its dogmas are nothing but recent (hence irrational) inventions, good only for the "oldies" and uncultured. Being irrational as it lacks tradition, Christianity, and nova religion, cannot claim to replace the religion of the fathers. Even Christian mythology, when compared to pagan mythology, appears absurd and meaningless. How is it possible, for example, to believe in the virgin birth of Jesus, about which Celsus writes: "Of being born of a virgin, you made it up. You were born in a village in Judea to a local woman, a poor day spinner. This one was cast out by her husband, a carpenter by profession, for proven adultery. Repudiated by her husband and reduced to ignominious vagrancy, clandestinely she gave birth to you by a soldier named Panther."[35]

But in addition to being irrational and immodest (that is, lacking the moderation that was a typical virtue of the philosopher), Christians are antisocial. Indeed, what could be more antisocial than refusing to make sacrifices to city deities and take an oath on the effigy of the emperor? Roman civil religion could not tolerate such acts without seeing in them an attack on social cohesion. And Celsus captures very well the anarchic and subversive character of Christianity. Here it is no longer a question of more or less reprehensible behavior such as donkey head worship. There is something more serious: by opposing philosophy and tradition, Christianity risks upsetting the centuries-old, shared value system that formed the cement of Roman society. Hence the need to oppose it on a philosophical level even before the courtrooms.

In 448, the Christian emperors Valentinian III and Theodosius II issued an edict in which they ordered, among other things, the burning of "all the works of Porphyry[36]". This speaks volumes about how later Christianity grasped the danger of Porphyry's Against Christians, so much so that the work was refuted by the best Christian pens (Eusebius of Caesarea, Jerome, and Augustine, to name but the best known).

---

[35] Celsus I,28, translated by G. Lanata, 1987
[36] Codex Iustinianus I,1,3

Effectively, this student of Plotinus, who lived in the second half of the iii century, in a temper characterized by a profound crisis affecting both material and immaterial realities, takes on an ambitious task: to demolish Christianity from the ground up by demonstrating its intrinsic irrationality. Wanting to employ modern terminology, one could say that in Porphyry, perhaps for the first time, the contrast between faith (pístis) and reason (lógos) is brought to the fore. There is a clear incompatibility -Porphyry says- between the irrationality of the Christian message, because of the popular character of its doctrinal apparatus that drives to superficial credulity and because of the lack of tradition, and the reasonableness of ancient philosophy. Moreover, Christians are atheists in that they reject traditional worship. Indeed, Porphyry asks, "How could those who have abandoned the patriarchal customs, by which the whole race and the whole state are held together, not be impious and atheistic? [...] Of what indulgence should those be deemed worthy who from time immemorial, among every people, Greek or barbarian, in the cities and the countryside, have kept away from temples, initiations, and mysteries?"

3.3 Instrumentalizations of myth: from storytelling to Nazi ideology

Bruce Lincoln, in *Theorizing Myth: Narrative, Ideology, and Scholarship*, points out that until the Renaissance there were attempts to rehabilitate the category of myth, but in most cases mythic narratives had lost their authoritative status, turning into fairy tales and folk tales, placed in opposition by Christians to the only story they considered authoritative: that of the Bible. With the texts recovered in the Renaissance, changes could finally be brought about by providing an alternative narrative to the main one given by the Church. A key text for this innovation was Tacitus' *Germania*, first made public in 1457 by Aeneas Silvius Piccolomini[37]

With the revival of Tacitus' text by Piccolomini (the future Pius II), the partisans of the empire focused on the passages where they idealized their ancestors, such as chapters 1-8 and 13-14 where the Germans' sense of honor and integrity, their physical prowess, courage and beauty, attachment to land and family, and especially the way they had defended their freedom against Rome were extolled. A few centuries after the discovery of this text, it was considered to be a historical event of considerable importance, so much so that it was compared to Columbus' discovery of America: if the latter had discovered a new world to the west, Tacitus had done an important service for the ancient northern world by breaking the Mediterranean monopoly on antiquities and giving the German, Scandinavian, Dutch, and Anglo-Saxon peoples a prestige derived from a deep and noble past. This feeling of pride, however, also prompted the production of texts that

---

[37] B. Lincoln, Theorizing Myth: Narrative, Ideology and Scholarship, Chicago, University of Chicago Press, 1999, p. 47.

would go on to exalt the past, and among the most enterprising we see Annio da Viterbo (Giovanni Nanni), who in 1512 published what he claimed to be a rediscovered manuscript of Berossus, a Babylonian prince; through this manuscript, a noble German culture was described, but this construction contained some detecting contradictions. This text, as unreliable as it was, triggered a nationalistic wave, which prompted many scholars to search for the ancient myths of their territories, sparking the writing of various collections of lost legends and epic poems, not only in German territories but in many other nations. These searches, in addition to nationalistic sentiment, stimulated, also, theoretical analyses at the center of which were ancient languages and legends. Among the most avid scholars was Johan Georg Hamann[38], who had a particular interest in language: he believed that each language carried within it the history of the people who spoke it, supporting and shaping their general worldview. Hamann was, however, a pietist pastor whose aim was to defend religion from the attacks that came from secular traditions; among his most faithful readers were authors such as Goethe, Kant, and Johan Gottfried Herder, also a pietist pastor who, starting from the multiplicity of species, came to support the difference with the equal dignity of all the *Völker* of the world, developing a relativist view.

The nationalism being created by the rediscovery of ancient traditions led thinkers to reflect on why over time the ability to transmit traditional knowledge had been lost. Herder responded to this by pointing out how modernity had caused the ancient oral customs to be forgotten; in this regard,

---

[38] Cf. I. Berlin, The Magus of the North. J.G. Hamann and the Origins of Modern Irrationalism, New York, Fer.

Wagner expressed himself, who advocated the emergence of a new kind of artistic production, one that would be characterized by the very voice of the *Volk* by proposing an example of a myth from which to draw inspiration in times of need: the story of Siegfried (Sigurd), dragon-slaying hero of the *Völsung* lineage. Wagner worked on this story for more than 30 years, expanding the fairy-tale sagamore and more, eventually writing the four dramas of the Ring cycle (*Bühnenfestspiel*), which then in 1848 became the author's first pseudo-academic treatise, in which fantasy and research met, entitled *The Wibelungen*; during the Middle Ages the power of German kings declined, but thanks to these writings about the past, the *Volk* were able to retain hope for the future. The fact that Wagner spoke of the German *Volk* and traced its origin to Asia was posited as the cause of the Aryan diaspora, which set the stage for his friendship with Count Artur de Gobineau, who was the first to formalize a systematic treatise on race (1853-55). At that time, racial theories were not widespread in Germany, but the scholar enthusiastically embraced them, making them more anti-Semitic and thus beginning the development of Nazi ideology. In the ideologies of the Third Reich, the division of "true" and "false," "good," and "bad" were used by the monotheistic colonizers when they forcefully imposed themselves on polytheistic religions, where the "bad guy" was embodied by the Jew, deformed in body, deprived of his language and land, i.e., the antithesis of what a true *Volk* should be. In the tradition, this opposition between the two peoples could only be resolved through what was called *Ragnarok*, which in the crude but effective propaganda of Nazism brought the Aryan discourse to disastrous consequences.

3.4 The militarization of a myth.

The involvement of myth in Aryan discourse, which began in the 9th century, also led to disastrous consequences from an academic point of view. Indeed, after World War II, work had to begin on restructuring the study of Indo-European myth, although it continued to be the focus of racist issues and publications of the "new right" for a long time to come. It was in this process of restructuring that the increasingly established figure of Georges Dumézil, whose studies were echoed by every author of that period, whose intent was to study the past without the influence of racial politics.

The scholar's goal in his research was to show that Indo-European peoples imagined an ideal social order where, as we have already seen in previous chapters, the three functions were integrated within a hierarchical system. We are witnessing work that is not without its critics, although it is said to have been completed without the influence of specific ideologies. Critics focused on the details of Dumèzel's studies of ancient sources, the scope of his comparative enterprise, his tendency to schematize, and his insistence that the tripartite model distinguished Indo-European peoples from all others. Yet, in the early 1980s, critics drew attention to the ideological positions to be perceived in his texts and sub-texts, emphasizing four key points:

1. The author's idealization of Indo-Europeans and their tripartition;

2. the fact that he introduced his theory of the three functions in his writings of 1938-42 when fascism was still a pressing concern for any Frenchman;

3. the similarity of this system to Mussolini's "corporate society" and Charles Maurras' "integral nationalism."

4. His involvement in circles close to Maurras' Action Française.

Some scholars pointed out an apparent "sympathy for Nazi culture" on Dumézil's part; his defenders opposed this view. Among the authors who sided with the scholar we also find the Parisian journalist Didier Eribon, who focuses his attention on the academic world in which Dumézil participated, highlighting how the intellectual environment of the 1920s and 1930s was a place where scholars with different ideological positions could dialogue and debate without having to contaminate the discourse with their political leanings: by doing so, hypothetically, those scholars would keep their professional judgment clean of what was out there.

We certainly realize that as attractive as this image may be, hardly credible. Political interests often played an important role in the discussion of Indo-European (or Aryan) religion and society, a condition that was not limited only to the German milieu, but went beyond the borders of Germany in the 1920s, 1930s, and '40. Just take as an example the work of Austrian folklorist Otto Höfler, who investigated the religious significance of martial bands, later deemed unbecoming of Nazism by Alfred Rosenberg (Hitler's main ideologue). This hostility on Rosenberg's part earned Höfler the support of Heinrich Himmler, who recruited him into the SS *Ahnenerbe* division, thereby securing a professorship in German philosophy at the University of Munich.

Eribon points out that in a collection of articles, written by Dumézil upon his return to France after teaching in Turkey and Sweden (thus dating back to 1933-35), it is clear that the author was a "pro-fascist and anti-Nazi" during the years he was writing, but the central question is whether Dumézil advanced these views in publications bearing his name or whether he "neutralized his political judgments about contemporary events because he was writing works of science." To clarify this point Lincoln examines Dumézil's interpretation of the god *Tyrin* in his 1940 volume *Mitra-Varuna*. Generally, the god is described as one who is "the boldest and bravest"

of the ancient Norse deities, as evidenced by the epithet "god of battle," the assimilation with the Roman Mars, and the use of the spear-shaped rune that bears his name as a spell for victory; while, on the contrary, Dumézil emphasizes the one myth that tells of *Týr*, preserved by Snorri in two variants, presenting *Odhinn as a* master of magic and *Týr* as a master of law. And it is precisely this interpretation of it that has sparked criticism, for if one goes to analyze other compositions from Germanic and Indo-European narrative culture, which have the same theme of the myth reported by Snorri and analyzed by Dumézil as their basis, one will notice that all these texts go on to describe how the hierarchical arrangement in three functions is inscribed on the body through a set of three wounds: a wound to the head or eye (*Odhinn*) signals those who are sovereigns; a wound to the hand or arm (*Týr*) signals those endowed with military power; wounded to the lower part of the body are those of low rank, whose appetites for food and wealth may be perceived as ignoble or dangerous, and who is reduced to positions of servile slavery.

To understand the reasons that led Dumézil to his interpretation we must rely on speculative theories. Dumézil addresses his first topic in *Mythes et dieux des Germains*, published in 1939 but written in 1936 when France was distressed by Hitler's rearmament of the Rhineland, the figure of *Odhinn* as a god with the inspirational force of the German nation and the Nazi movement. The author had observed that the Romans, Celts, and Indo-Iranians possessed strong and conservative priestly institutions, while the absence of these institutions among the Germans allowed for a distinct "slippage" in their mythology, making it different from all other Indo-European peoples. The scholar intended to relieve Indo-Europeans of responsibility for German militarism and to blame it on the Germans' deviation from their Indo-European ideals. To achieve this end Dumézil argues that the Germans weakened their royal and priestly institutions with the result that they were unable to curb the violence of their warriors. To confirm this thesis he posits *Odhinn*, head of the pantheon, as a terrifying war chief, emphasizing the "militarization" of German mythology.

In contrast to the Greek, Roman, and Celtic myths that initiated Christian conversion, Germanic stories survived in a myriad of heroic legends that were ready to be revived by the Romantics, Wagner, and other artists. Consequently, the Third Reich did not have to create myths, but on the contrary, it was Germanic mythology, resurrected in the 19th century, that gave form, spirit, and institutions to a Germany whose evils were conceived by Hitler within the fabled realm of *Odhinn*.

CONCLUSIONS

The study of the religion of the Germans is severely conditioned by the scarcity and problematic nature of the sources available to us. In this context, the present paper aimed to move between history and historiography, integrating into the analysis of Georges Dumézil's studies of Germanic mythology and the criticisms made of him, and emphasizing the importance of antiquity of what we now call myths, fables, and children's tales.

The religious culture of the Germans, unlike that of the Greeks and Romans, is little known among the masses and has been introduced into Pop culture only through movies, novels, and in recent years TV series that feature historical and mythological inaccuracies, and, of course, poetic licenses. In the common consciousness, because of these passive means of learning, the so-called Viking (or Scandinavian) culture is often linked to Nazism because of the symbols that the Nazis used in their propaganda and that today the collective imagination associates with the ancient Germanic peoples. The rediscovery of their religious universe in the light of a critical study of documentary sources, as well as of the historiography and ideology they produced and nurtured while being themselves altered and distorted, therefore proves to be an essential tool for historical and philosophical self-awareness.

Thank you for getting to the end of the book, I have spent a lot of time writing the manuscript and I ask you to help me with the dissemination of the book. It would be very helpful if you would leave me a positive review on AMAZON. Thank you very much!

BIBLIOGRAPHY

Primary bibliography

Adam Di Bremen, *History of the Archbishops of the Church of Hamburg*, Turin, Utet, De Agostini Libri, 2013.

Snorri Sturluson, *Edda,* edited by Giorgio Dolfini, Milan, Adelphi, 2019.

Secondary bibliography

I. Berlin, *The Magus of the North. J.G. Hamann and the Origins of Modern Irrationalism*, New York, Ferrar, Straus, and Giroux, 1993.

B. Bettelheim, *The Uses of Enchantment. The Meaning and Importance of Fairy Tales*, New York, Knopf, 1976.

M. Bettini, *In Praise of Polytheism. What we can learn today from ancient religions*, Bologna, il Mulino, 2014.

Ph. Borgeaud, F. Prescendi (eds.), *Ancient Religions. A comparative introduction*, transl. en., Rome, Carocci, 2011.

Castrucci, *The historical-anthropological reassessment of the Indo-European past*, in *La teoria indoeuropea delle tre funzioni in Georges Dumézil e altri saggi. Reconnaissance for a critique of culture*, Milan, Giuffrè, 2019.

G. Dumézil, *El destino del guerrero*, translated by Juan Almela, México, Siglo XXI Editores, 1971.

G. Dumézil, *The Gods of the Germans*, translated by Bianca Candian, Milan, Adelphi, 2019.

G. Dumézil, *Loki,* Darmstadt, Wissenschaftliche Buchgesellschaft, 1959.

Dumézil, *Mitra-Varuna. Essai sur deux représentations indo-européennes de la souveraineté*, Paris, Presses universitaires de France, 1940.

D. Eribon, *Faut-il brûler Dumézil?* , Paris, Flammarion, 1992.

C. Ginzburg, *Germanic Mythology and Nazism. On an old book by Georges Dumézil,*

"Historical Notebooks" 57/3, 1984, pp. 857-882.

J. and W. Grimm, *Princess mouse hair and 41 other fairy tales to be discovered* (1818), Rome, Donzelli, 2012.

C. Grottanelli, *Ideologies, myths, massacres. Indo-Europeans by Georges Dumézil*, Palermo, Sellerio, 1993.

B. Lincoln, *Death, War, and Sacrifice: Studies in Ideology and Practice*, Chicago, University of Chicago Press, 1991.

B. Lincoln, *Theorizing Myth: Narrative, Ideology and Scholarship*, Chicago, University of Chicago Press, 1999.

A. Momigliano, *Premises for a discussion of Georges Dumézil*, "Opus" 2, 1983, pp. 329-341.

V.J. Propp, *Morphology of the Fairy Tale*, edited by G.L. Bravo, Turin, Einaudi, 2000.

J.R.R. Tolkien, *Tree and Leaf,* translated in Italian by Francesco Saba Sardi, Milan, Bompiani, 2004 (ed. or. London 1964).

Made in United States
Troutdale, OR
12/08/2023